SCHLOSS DRACHENBURG
in the Siebengebirge

Deutscher Kunstverlag Berlin München

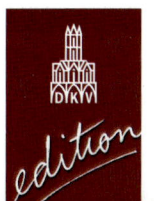

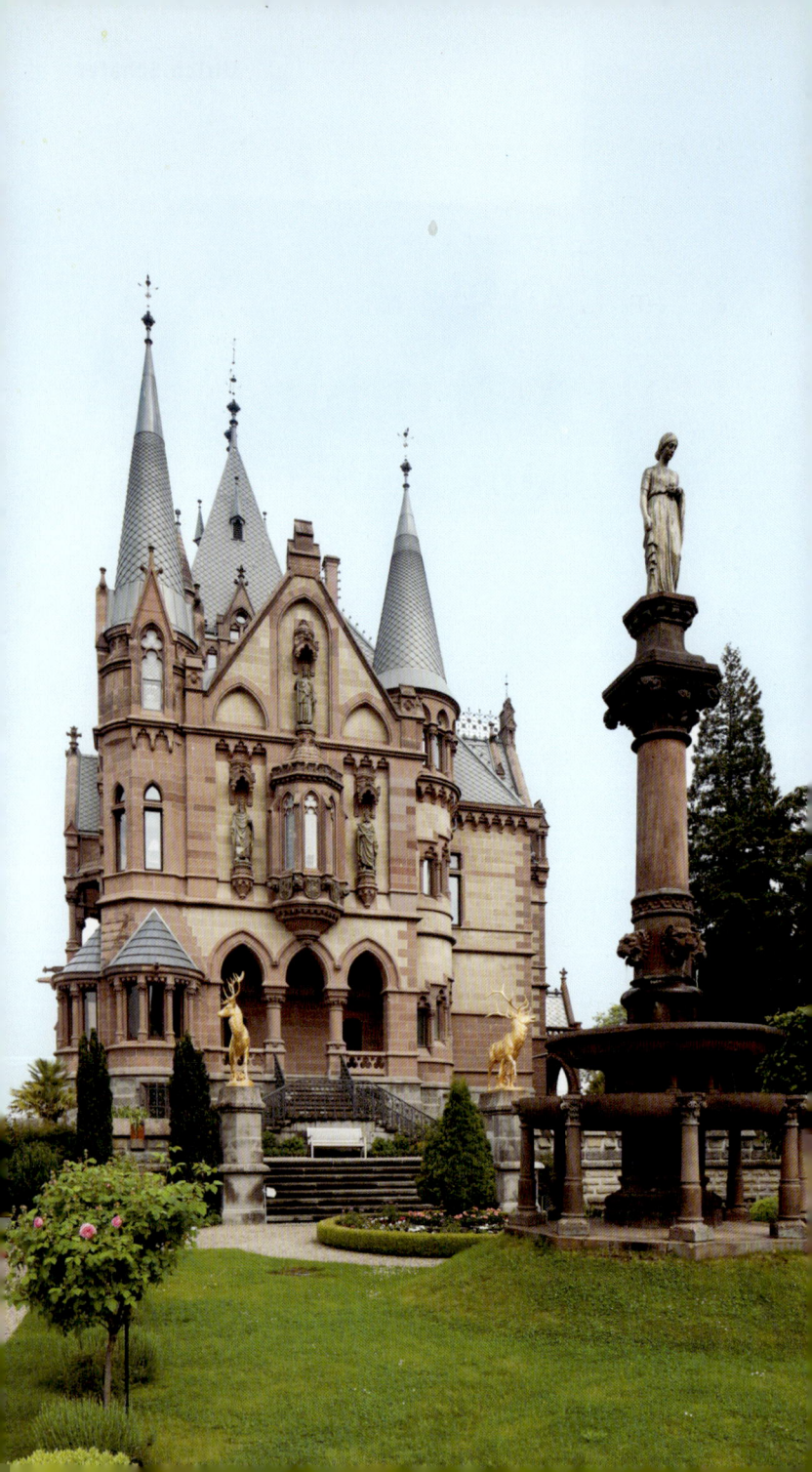

CONTENTS

- 4 PRELUDE
- 10 APPROACHING SCHLOSS DRACHENBURG
- 16 THE PALACE BUILDINGS
- 16 **The Vorburg (Front Building)**
- 19 **The Main Building**
- 28 **The Architectural Sculpture**
- 39 THE INTERIORS
- 39 **Main Entrance, Vestibule, and Stairwell**
- 47 **Reception Hall**
- 48 **Dining Room**
- 51 **Nibelung Room**
- 54 **Art Gallery**
- 58 **Tavern Room**
- 63 **Billiard Room**
- 63 **Library**
- 66 **Music Hall**
- 69 **Private Residential Quarters**
- 72 **Guest-of-Honour Quarters**
- 77 THE HISTORY OF THE DRACHENBURG
- 82 THE MONUMENT SCHLOSS DRACHENBURG
- 88 THE NRW FOUNDATION
- 93 LITERATURE · ADDRESSES
- 94 PUBLISHING DETAILS

Venus Terrace and South Facade

PRELUDE

On the western slope of the Drachenfels, the "Dragon's Rock", facing the Rhine, in the middle of the beautiful Siebengebirge landscape, stands a building which, with its picturesque wealth of detail, is impressive even from a distance. Viewed from the north, the hills of the Central German Uplands merge here. And here, geographically, the Middle Rhine Gorge – which already attracted tourists in the eighteenth century with its 'castle romanticism' – begins (or ends, following the flow of the river). Lord Byron, Heinrich Heine, William Turner, and many other artists found inspiration here for some of best works.

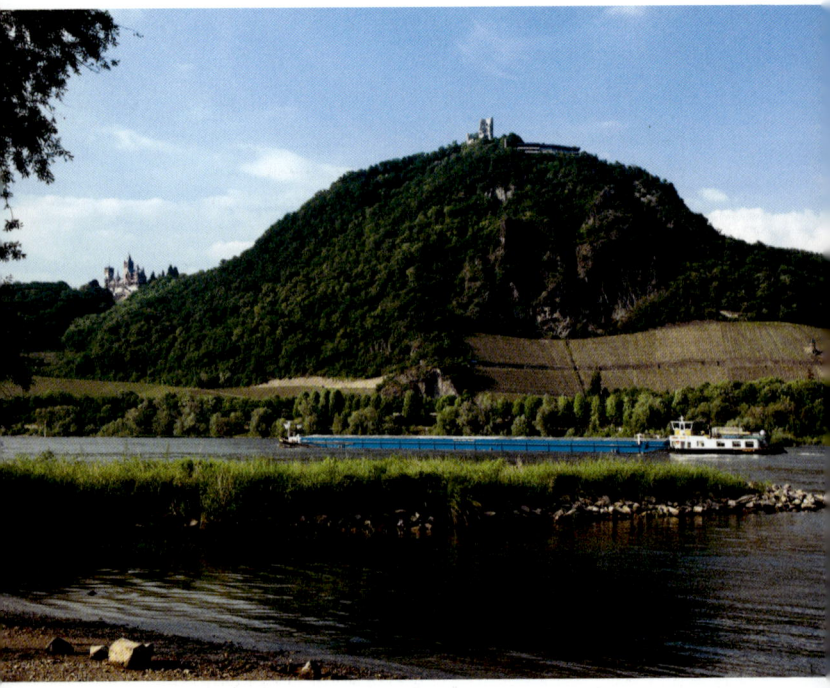

View over the Rhine of the Drachenfels and Drachenburg

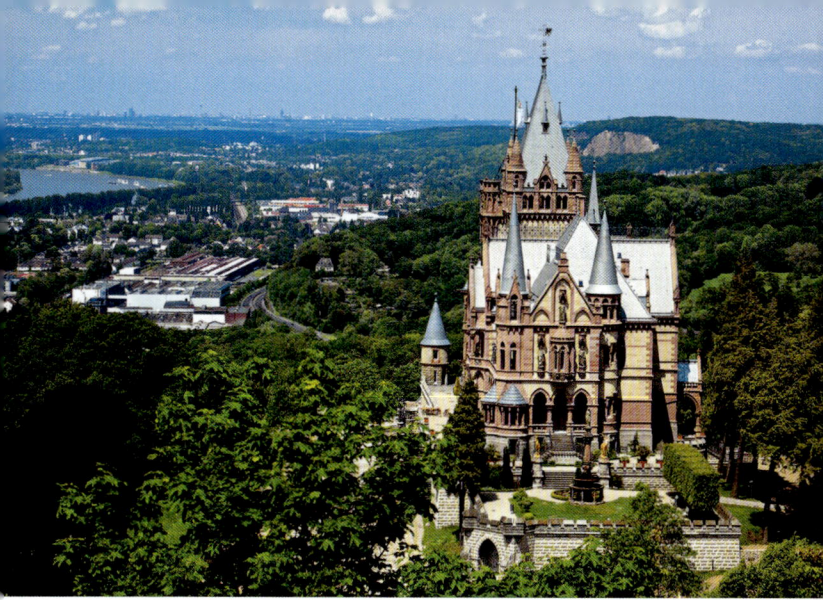

View from the Vista Point on the way up to the Drachenfels

But Schloss Drachenburg (Drachenburg castle) itself in this highly impressive setting is a creation of the late nineteenth century. Several centuries separate it from the ruin on the Drachenfels and the many other castle ruins along the Rhine. Unlike Bavaria's Neuschwanstein, no king built this "Neuschwanstein of the Rhine region", but rather a veritable self-made man, the Baron Stephan von Sarter, who had humble roots and had earned his fortune abroad, on the stock market. Born in Bad Godesberg and brought up in Cologne, he had found success in Paris (see p. 6/7).

King Ludwig II's castle project in Bavaria is likely to have inspired Stephan Sarter. The son of a commoner, he was ennobled in 1881, when the Duke of Saxony-Meiningen conferred the title of *Freiherr*, or baron, upon him. Contracted by Sarter and built from 1882 to 1884, Schloss Drachenburg was intended to be a dignified backdrop for himself as a baron. However, he never lived in his castle. Still a bachelor, he remained in Paris, the city of his successes, until his death in 1902.

Baron Stephan von Sarter (Bonn 1833 – 1902 Paris)

Stemming from a less than well off family in Bonn, Stephan Sarter left high school after secondary school to do an apprenticeship at Cologne's Leopold Seligmann Bank. Recommended by his instructor, he changed over to the Salomon Oppenheim Bank in 1856, which in turn soon transferred him to their Paris branch.

Stephan Sarter developed into an expert in stock market transactions. His specialty was the assessment of bonds and market-listed companies: the job description of today's financial analysts. In the nineteenth century, it was imperative to travel in order to research the credit-worthiness of stock companies. The Paris stock market also traded stocks of foreign companies, such as, for instance, railway stock from the United States, Spain, or Austria.

Stephan Sarter was able to successfully use the insight he gained from his analyses for his own speculative trading and his employment supplied him with sufficient capital to invest. He was thus able to become self-employed in 1862: he began publishing his analyses in brochures and magazines, and speculated independently. He was especially successful as an adventurer in stocks for the Suez Canal Company, which he also repeatedly recommended for purchase in his brochures, making sure to mention his previous accurate prognoses.

There are no direct sources regarding the extent of the fortune he amassed in this way. But the buildings and landscaped gardens of Schloss Drachenburg speak for themselves: Sarter sank a lot of money into his everlasting renown. Likewise, Sarter's promotion to nobility in 1881 cost him money as well. Toward the end of the century, his business activities were no longer going as well. He had made bad speculations and apparently lost part of his fortune. But he was never in such financial straits that he would have had to sell the Drachenburg.

The construction of the Drachenburg shines an oddly dichotomous light on its owner. He had spent much money to present himself as a German baron rooted to his homeland and its myths. Simultaneously, he was successfully moving forward with his French naturalization: Sarter became a Frenchman in 1890. He never lived in the Drachenburg. He died in 1902 in Paris; his grave is at the cemetery in Königswinter, right below the Drachenburg.

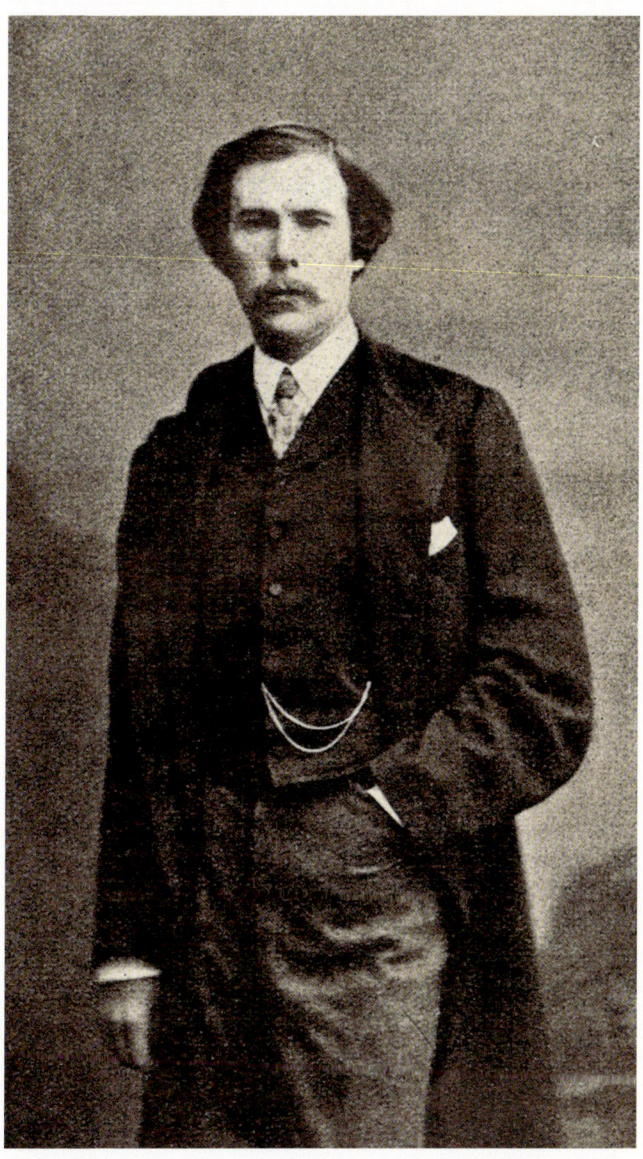

Stephan Sarter, reproduction from J. H. Biesenbach, "A Rhenish Youth", photo 1858

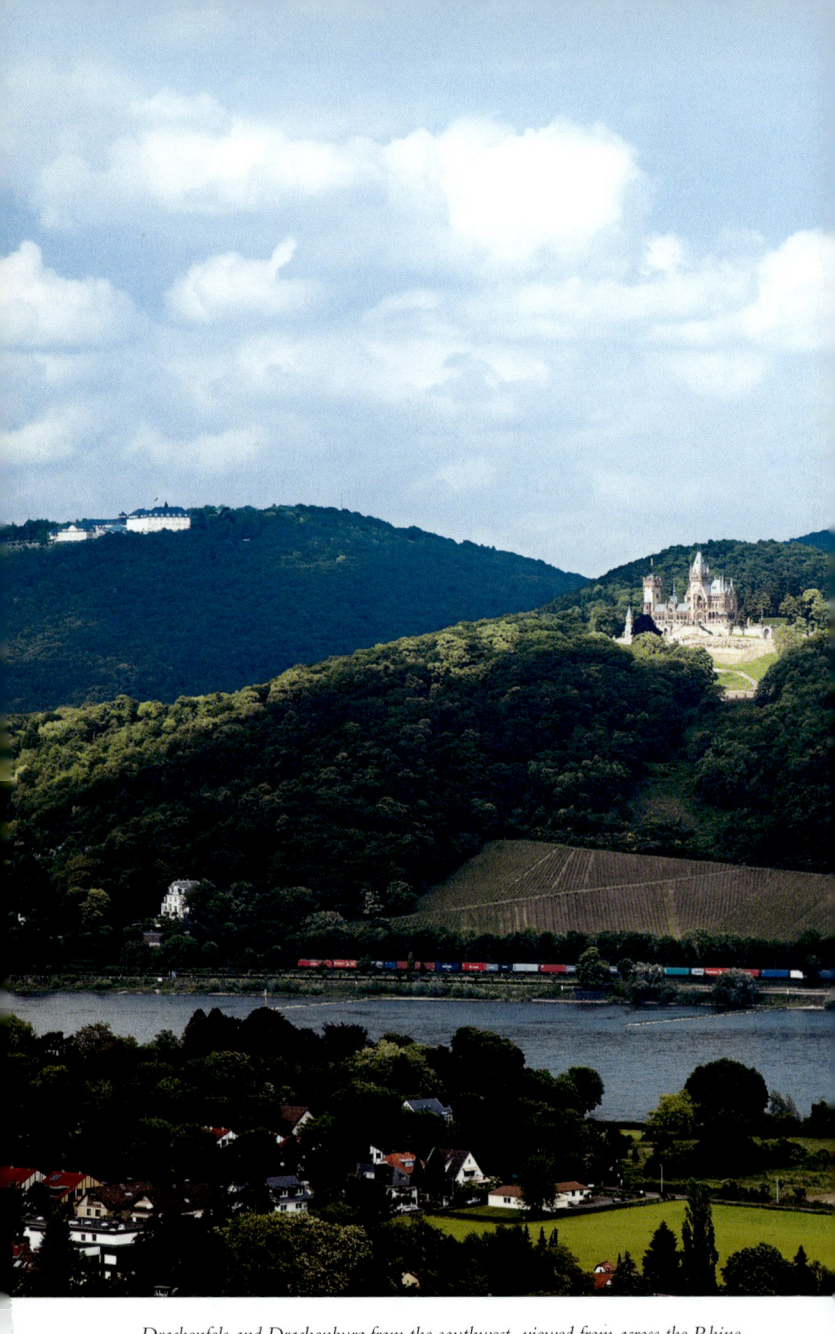
Drachenfels and Drachenburg from the southwest, viewed from across the Rhine,

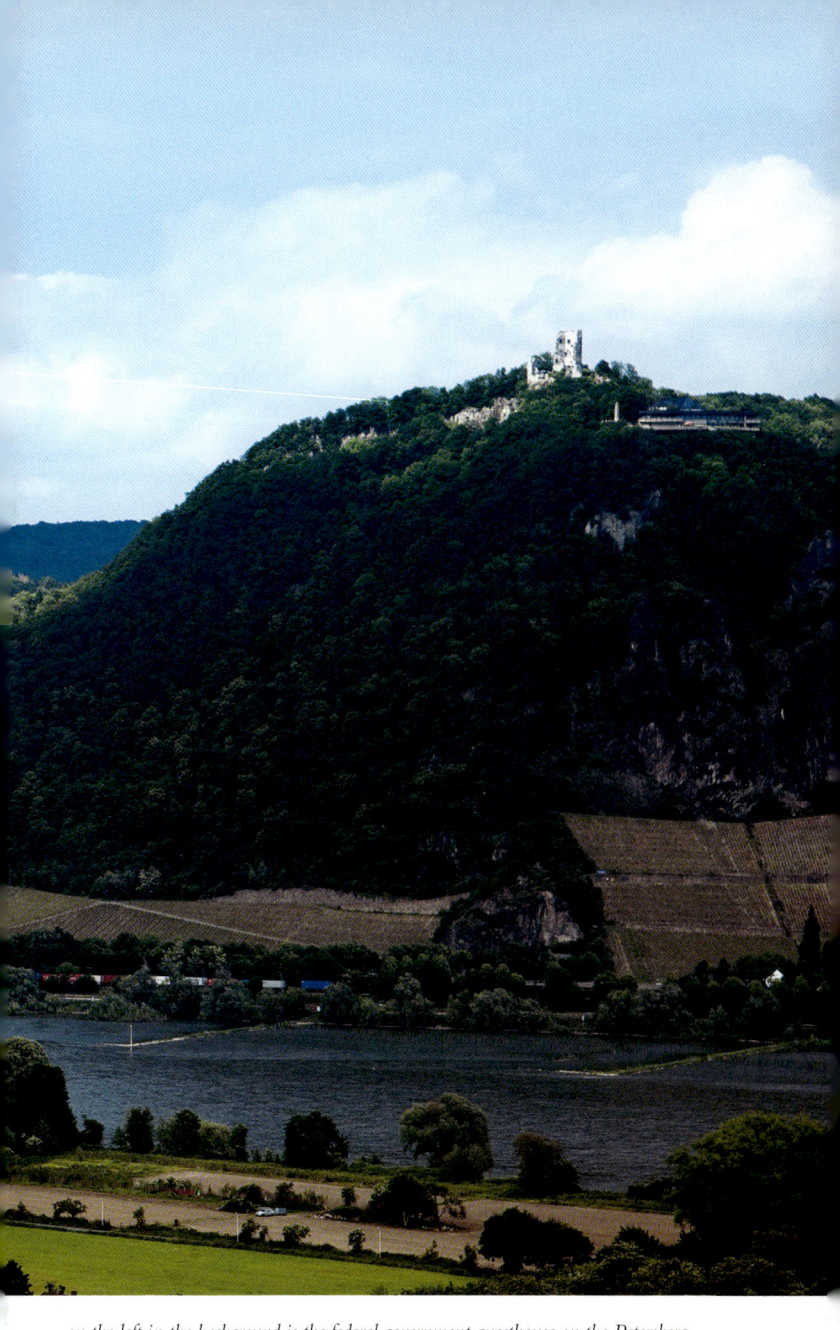

on the left in the background is the federal government guesthouse on the Petersberg

APPROACHING SCHLOSS DRACHENBURG

Since the eighteenth century – and to this day – the narrow middle reaches of the Rhine, with its peaks, castles, and ruins hugging its banks, have been perceived as highly romantic. The landscape attracted travellers, even becoming an obligatory part of the "grand tour" popular with the young British nobility. With its ambience and emotional connotations, the area kindled the imagination of poets and painters alike.

The Drachenfels stood out from its environment as a particularly special place. Lord Byron (*The Castled Crag of Drachenfels*), Heinrich Heine, Ferdinand Freiligrath, and many other poets have found inspiration in this setting, with its landscape and

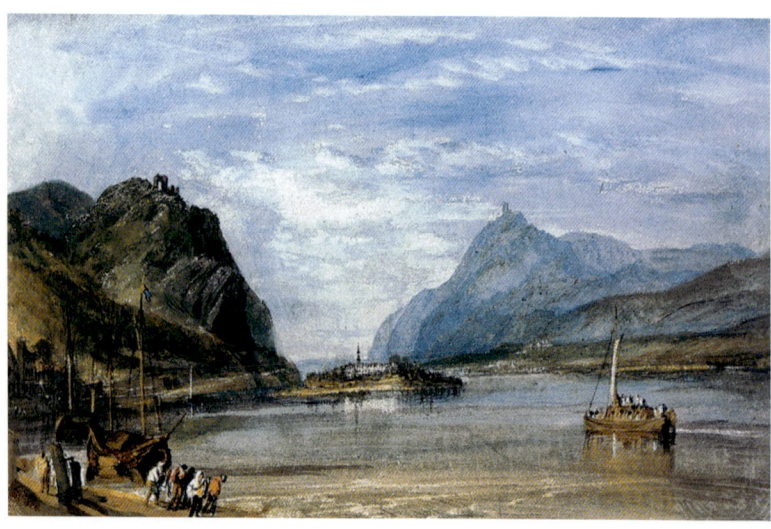

Joseph Mallord William Turner, Drachenfels and Roland's Arch from the south, 1817, Tate Britain, London

APPROACHING SCHLOSS DRACHENBURG

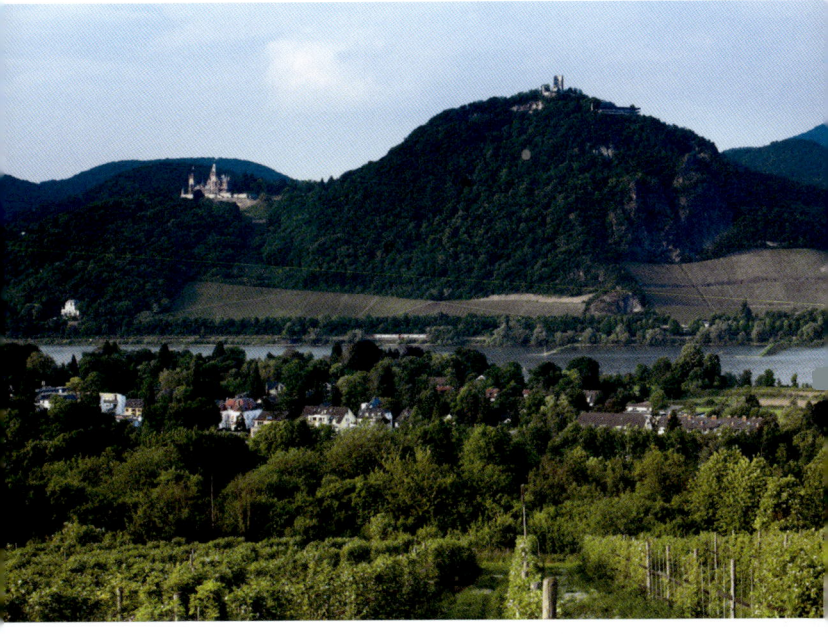

"Heinrich's View", located between Mehlem and Niederbachen

the prominently situated castle ruin. For many painters – William Turner repeatedly, for example – the view from the south onto Drachenfels and Roland's Arch was a stimulating motif (image p. 10). Stephan Sarter had succeeded in purchasing an extended piece of property below the Drachenfels in order to insert his castle into this panorama.

The distant view that Turner and many others preferred from the south or south-southwest shows the Main Tower and the Northern Tower in clear hierarchy. The roof-scape to the south of the Main Tower and the dome over the Art Gallery between the Main Tower and the North Tower can also be seen clearly. Steep roofs and several trees jut out from the curving horizon of the Central German Uplands. "Heinrich's View" – a vista point

APPROACHING SCHLOSS DRACHENBURG

between Mehlem and Niederbachem – reveals more of the palace's substructure (image p. 11). From the Petersberg one can see the Front Building as well, behind which the palace's towers and roofs tower up impressively (image on the front cover flap).

Somewhat closer vista points include the view from the Monument for Heinrich von Dechen and a scenic outlook halfway between the Drachenburg and the Drachenfels castle ruin (see cover picture). From the Dechen Monument, one can spot spires jutting up from behind treetops above the Front Building (image p. 14/15). The view from the outlook halfway between the peak with the ruin and the Drachenburg is spectacular. From here one can see the southern façade with the Venus Terrace (image p. 5). This perspective offers a lovely view of the edifice against the

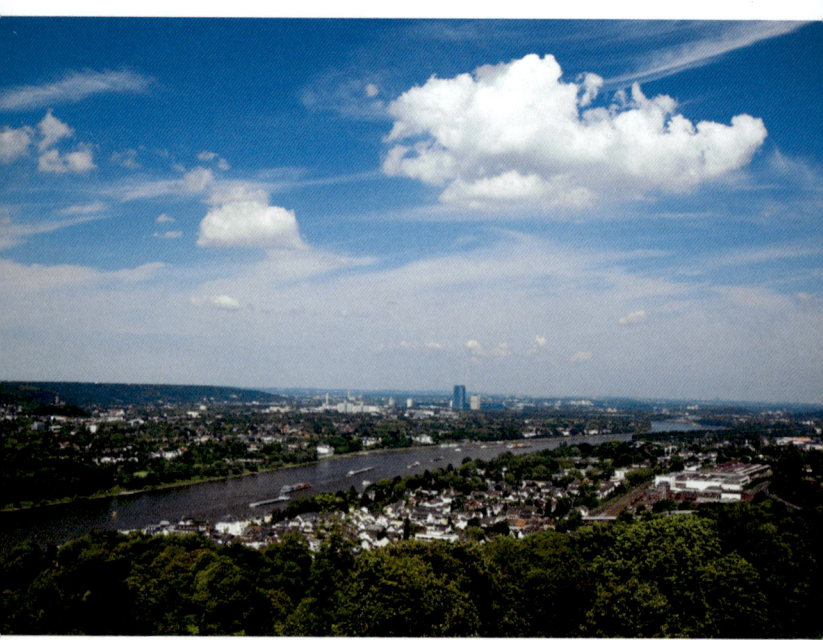

View northwards from the Drachenfels

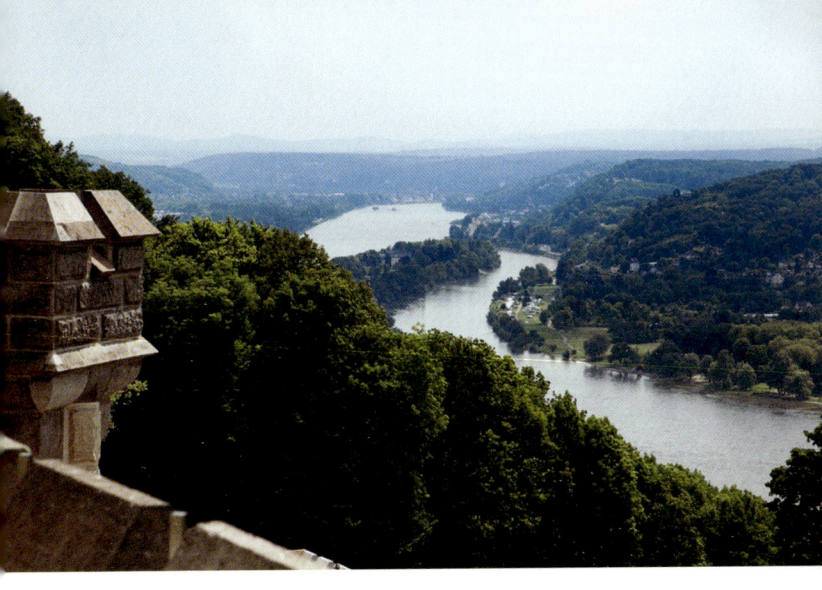

View southwards from the Venus Terrace with the Rhine and the island of Nonnenwerth

background of the river valley as it widens toward the north – an area that is quite spoiled by urban sprawl and marked by not exactly attractive industrial areas.

This elevated position on high also boasts beautiful views in the other direction. On very clear days, one can see from the Northern Tower's terrace all the way to Cologne (image p. 12), and a closer look reveals that the longitudinal walls are aligned with the towers of the Cologne Cathedral. From the Venus Terrace the view includes the Rhine at Bad Honnef with the island Nonnenwerth (image above). This view can of course also be seen from the towers and various alcoves.

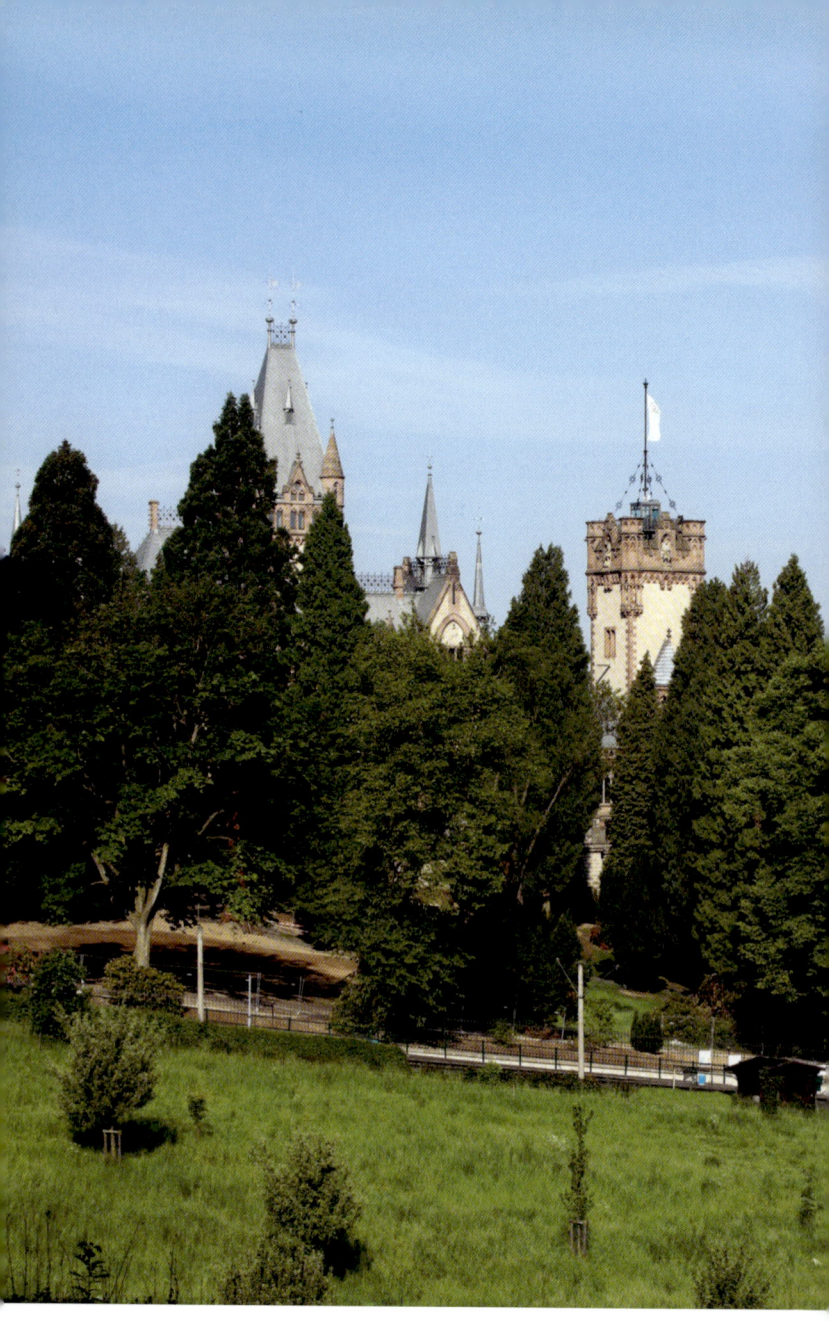
View from the Dechen Monument

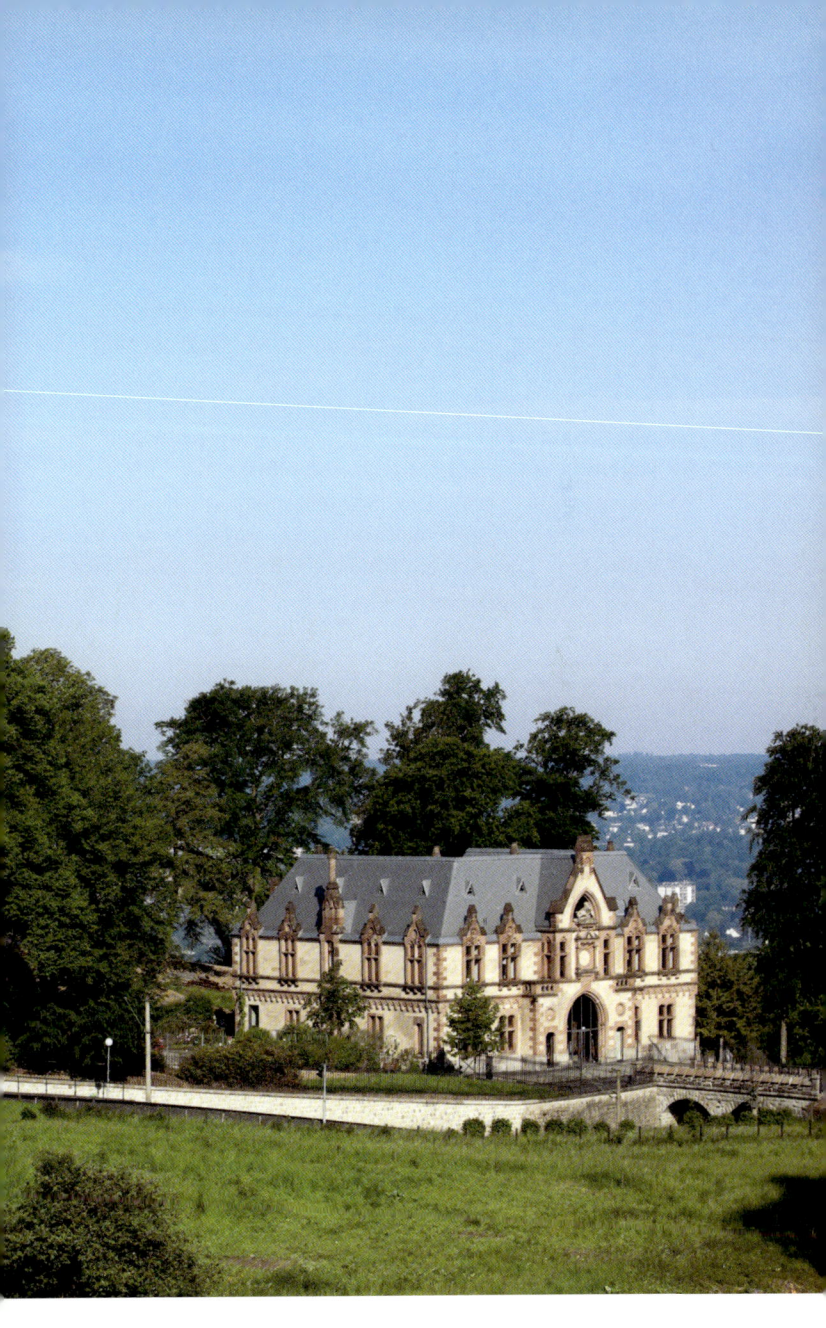

THE PALACE BUILDINGS

The Vorburg (Front Building)

The carefully staged entry to the expansive castle precinct begins at the Front Building. The ogival opening in the accented middle of the central wing used to be the entrance to the compound. Through this gate, the carriage reached the inner courtyard of the Front Building, which is flanked by the side wings of the consistently symmetrical three-wing-construction. From there one proceeded further. Today this ogival opening has a glass door and visitors are led through the shop in the southern side wing and on into the inner courtyard,

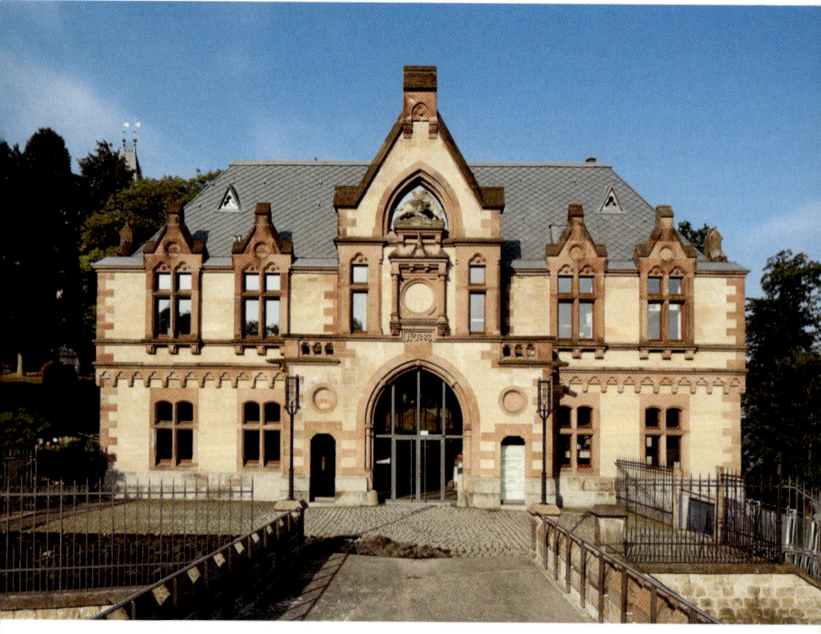

Eastern view of the Front Building

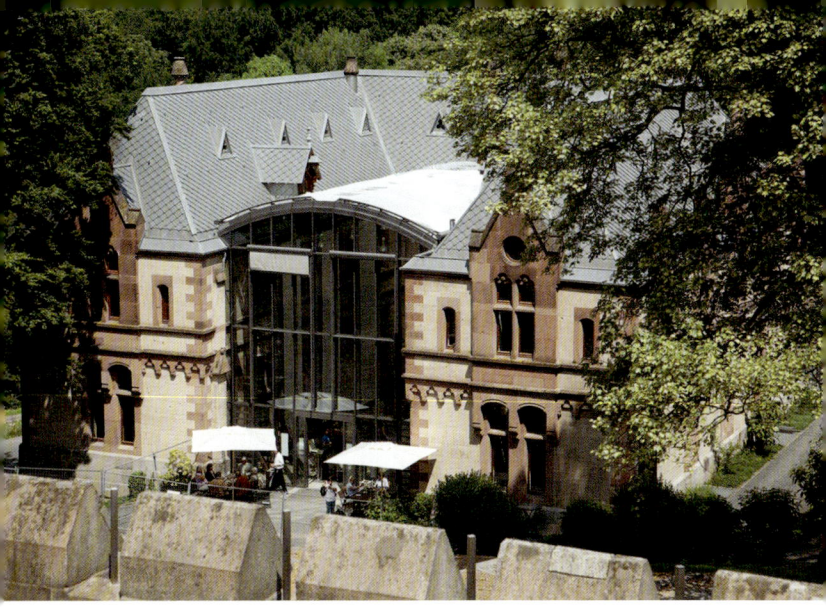

Southwestern view of the Front Building

which is now covered with a glass roof. From here, visitors have the opportunity to visit the Museum for the History of Nature Conservation, which is housed on both floors of the northern wing. The management for both the Foundation for Nature Conservation and the Drachenburg are located in the upper floor of this wing as well (see p. 18).

The Front Building's eastern façade, which faces visitors approaching the castle via the carriage path, is accentuated with a median avant-corps, the gabled muntin windows on the upper floor, the trefoil arch frieze between the two stories, and other ornamental elements. The sides are only slightly sleeker (image p. 19). The segmental arch-style glass roof covering the inner courtyard is attached above the eaves. This and the glass wall to the west allow for an unobstructed view of the original elements (image above). The facades of the Front Building are strictly symmetrical.

Foundation, Archive, Forum, and Museum for the History of Nature Conservation

The Drachenfels is considered to be one of the origins of nature Conservation in Germany. For centuries stone was quarried here, for the St. Victor's Church in Xanten and the Cologne Cathedral, among others. The latter's construction in the Gothic style had been at a standstill since the sixteenth century. Between the choir and the transept in the east and the towers that had been started in the west, lay the old Romanesque nave. When the building plans were discovered in the 1820s, construction began again in response to a civic initiative. At this time, the old stone quarries on the Drachenfels were reactivated. But here too civic initiative was sparked: in this case, with the intent to prevent the mountain from being carried off and the castle ruins destroyed. Interestingly enough, both initiatives were supported by the Prussian state, which gave massive support to the construction of the Cologne Cathedral and purchased Drachenfels. The builders had to find other sources for their materials.

In 1996, when the states North Rhine-Westphalia (NRW) and Brandenburg, as well as the "NRW Foundation for Nature Conservation, the Preservation of Local Customs and Traditions, and Culture", established the Foundation for Natural History, one of the things they had in mind was the Siebengebirge, Germany's oldest nature reserve. Accordingly, the Drachenburg's Front Building was the perfect location: the foundation was looking for a home and the Front Building needed a use. The Drachenfels, Schloss Drachenburg, the Museum for Nature Conservation, and other institutions, like the Nibelung Hall, reciprocally supply each other with visitors.

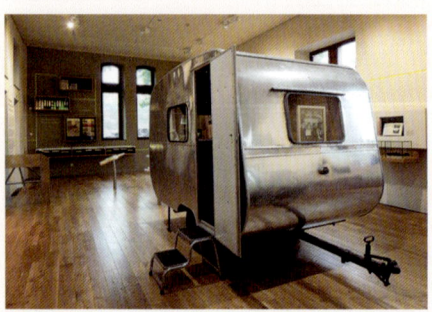

The Museum for the History of Nature Conservation

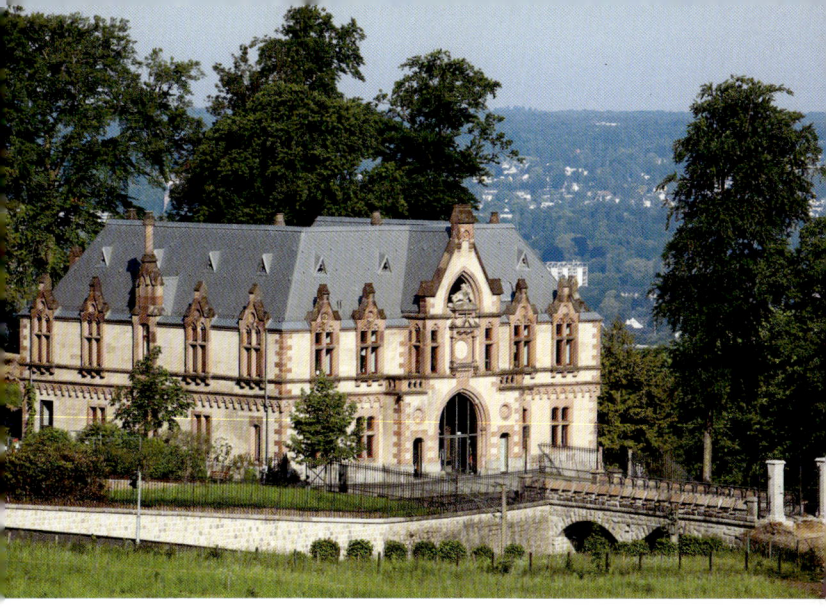

Southeastern view of the Front Building

The Main Building

The main building is symmetrical only in its details. A visitor approaching the castle from the Front Building has a low-angle view of a fairly unbalanced construction, which does not appear to have any axis of symmetry. Towers, small towers, alcoves, steep roofs, gables, dormers, staircases, and terraces impede anyone viewing the outside from understanding the building's structure (image p. 21).

An expansive base designed as a terrace connects the building with the landscape. Seen from below, this base is a rough, crenelated rustic wall. Its crenelation gives the impression of strong fortification. But the open staircase to a semi-circular protrusion on the western side and the ovigal portals to the lower parts of the palace on the western and northern sides reduce this to absurdity. In these ways the castle is clearly a product of the Wilhelminian period, when playing with motifs from the Middle Ages was popular.

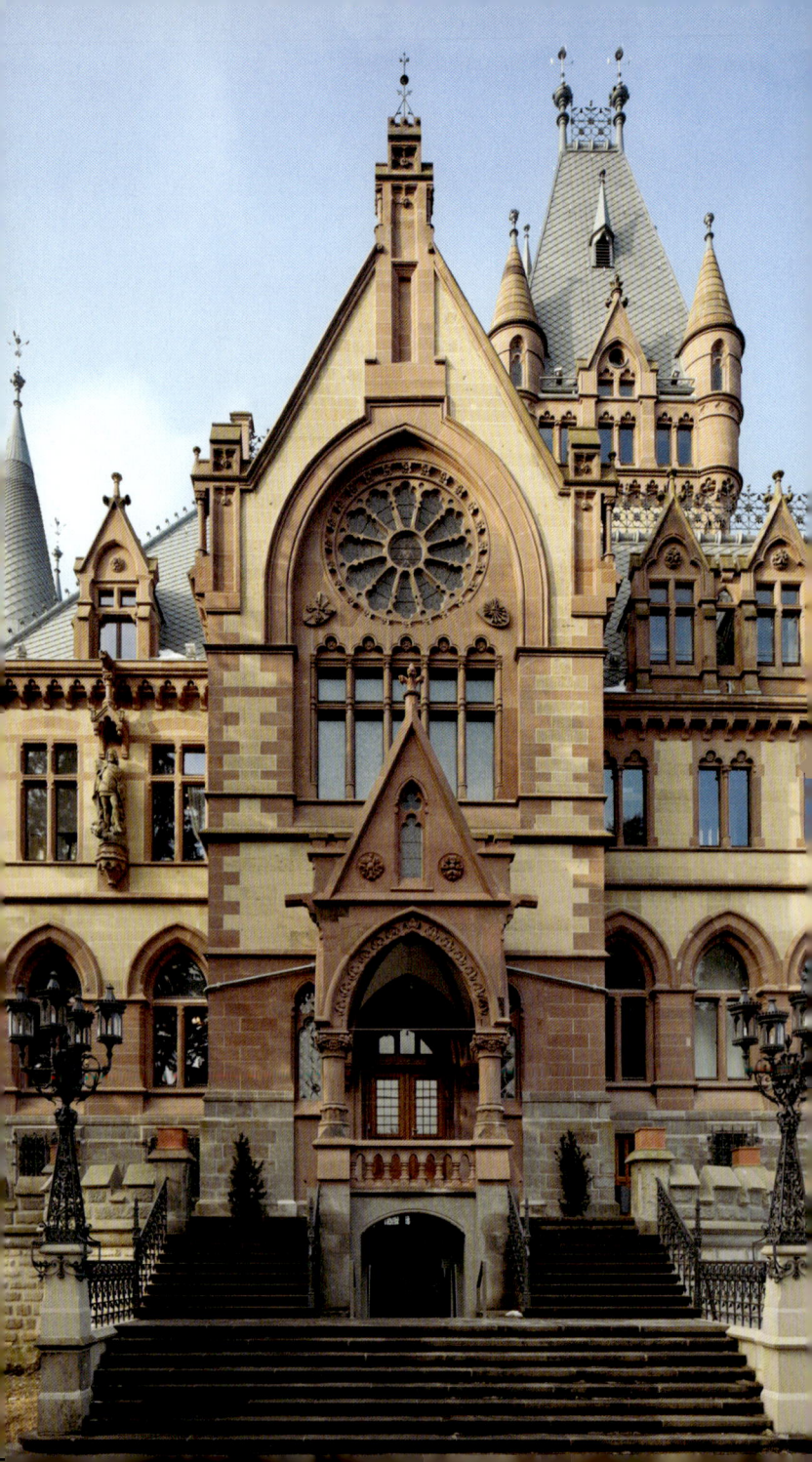

THE PALACE BUILDINGS

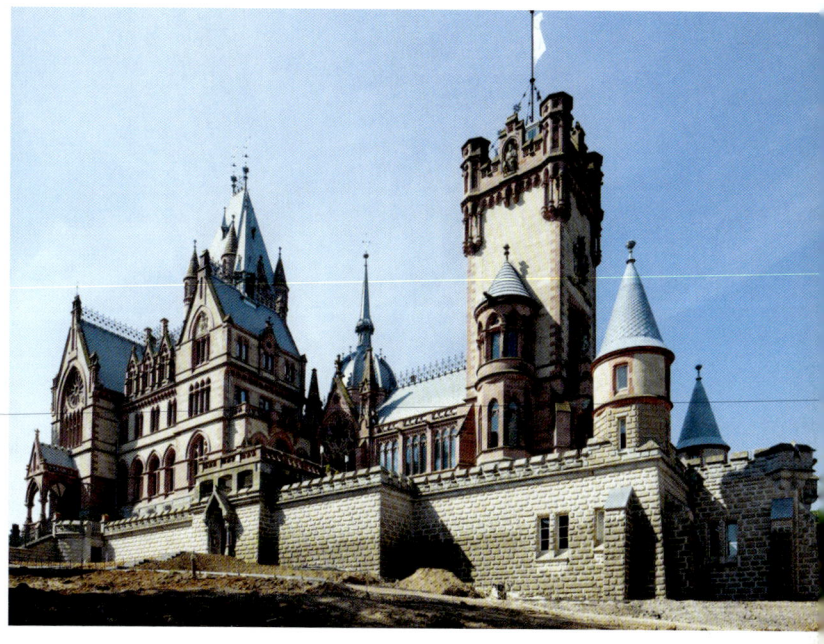

Schloss Drachenburg from the northeast

Via a further outdoor staircase on the eastern side (see image on left) a visitor coming from the Front Building reaches the terrace, which surrounds the entire building, and the portico in front of the main entrance.

Rising up over a grey-veneered high cellar or base story, is the two-story core building with its opulent roof-scape. The outer walls of the two residential and representational floors have a yellow veneer, while the pilaster strips, arches, corners, friezes, corbels, columns, and sills are accentuated with reddish stone. On the mountain side of the castle, a façade, led to by an open staircase, which at the top leads as a double staircase to the main entrance, juts out of the wall line: it has a high gable, a five-part window topped by a tracery rosette, and a small entrance hall. Behind this façade are a Vestibule and a stairwell.

The southern portion of the east facade

THE PALACE BUILDINGS

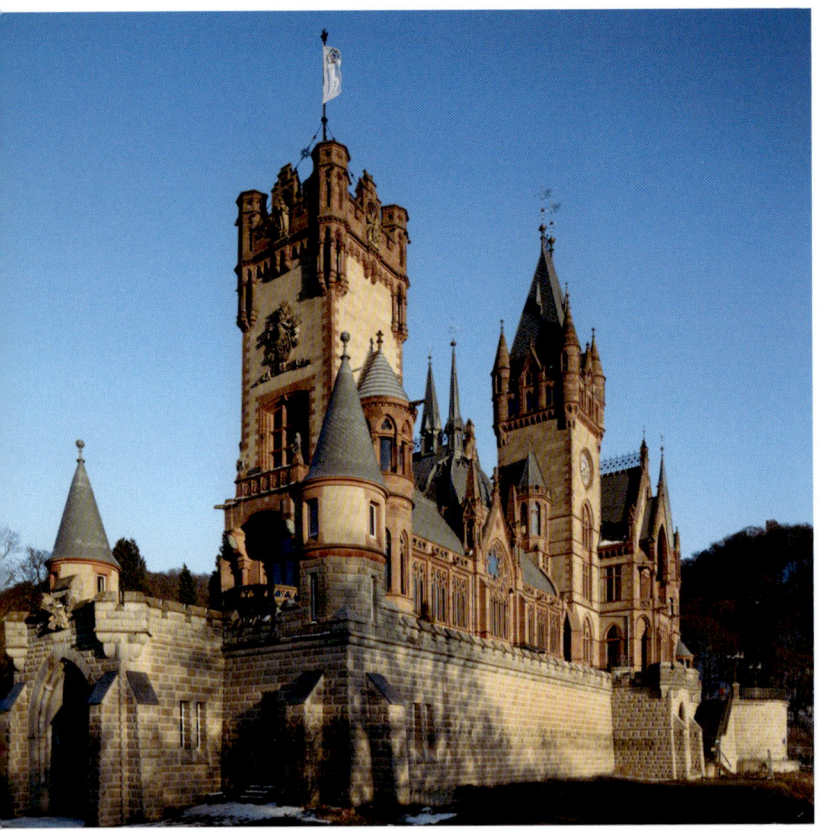

View of the Drachenburg from the northwest, from the hillside lawn

An equivalent to this protruding façade, with different aesthetic elements, can be found on the western side facing the Rhine valley. The high gables of the two protrusions are connected in the roof-scape by a continuous ridge. On the western side there is the Reception Hall and above it the Music Hall, both of which are accentuated in the outer building and, as the most important representational rooms, are connected directly to the stairwell.

The Architects of the Drachenburg

Very little documentation remains from the time of construction. Most sources are second hand, from magazines and newspapers. Three plans dated 1881, from the Düsseldorf architecture studio of Bernhard Tüshaus (1846–1909) and his brother-in-law Leo von Abbema (1852–1929), show three of the castle's facades – east, west (image p. 24), and south – and a cross-section of the building at the level of the Main Stairwell, the Reception Hall, and the Music Hall. These plans even begin to display details of the permanent wall fixtures of the northern walls of these rooms. Unfortunately, the page with the cross-section and the southern façade is a diazo copy of a drawing and is consequently not as well preserved as the other two, which are pen drawings.

The façade sketches show Schloss Drachenburg in an early stage of the project in which the Art Gallery and the North Tower are still missing. Unfortunately an outline of the northern side is missing. This is where the most changes occurred in contrast to the early plans of 1881.

The sixth issue of the third 1887 volume of the *Architektonische Rundschau*, published by Ludwig Eisenlohr and Carl Weigle, states: "Regarding the interior configuration, the architect and the owner unfortunately had different opinions, in response to which a large part of the work was transferred to the architect Hoffmann in Paris".

We know very little about Wilhelm Hoffmann, not even his dates of birth and death. However, his training at the Cologne Cathedral construction office and his later move to Paris fit to the Drachenburg's owner, who surely observed the advancement of the cathedral's construction during his apprenticeship in Cologne and later moved to the metropolis on the Seine, just like the architect.

In the *Frankfurter Zeitung*, dated September 24, 1884, Johannes Proelß even writes about a complete reworking of the plans created by the architects in Düsseldorf, undertaken by Wilhelm Hoffmann. This certainly refers to the building plans, and Angelika Schyma even credits the Parisian architect Wilhelm Hoffmann entirely for the Northern Tower and for the Art Gallery, which connects to the building designed by Tüshaus and von Abbema on the northern side.

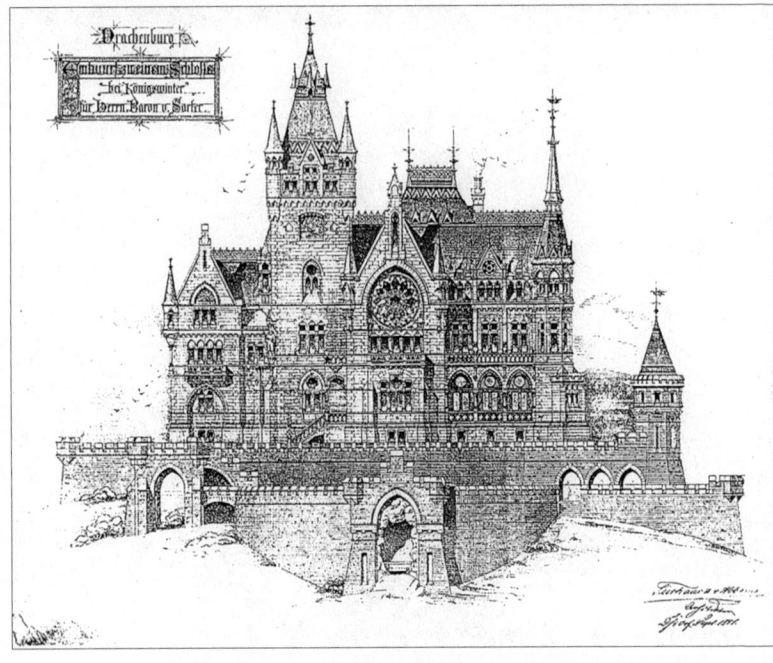

Architecture Firm Tüshaus & von Abbema, 1881, Drachenburg project, view from the west

The work at the construction site in Königswinter was overseen by Franz Langenberg (1842–1895), the son of an old family of master-builders from the lower Rhine. He created the designs for the wall and the ceiling ornamentation, which show a thorough understanding of the furniture of the fifteenth and sixteenth century.

We do not know anything about the designer of the remarkable park, which mediates sensitively between the architecture and the surrounding nature.

The Drachenburg's Landscape Park

Specialists refer to the expansive outdoor installations surrounding Schloss Drachenburg as a "zoned landscape garden". In this concept, developed in the nineteenth century, the intensity of landscape manipulation decreases the farther one moves from the residential structure. Thus, at some distance from the residence, the garden smoothly transitions into nature.

The direct surroundings of Schloss Drachenburg include the terraces, which are stylistically aligned with the buildings with their small towers, crenelations, abutments, and stairs. With their lawns, flowerbeds, and plants, they connect elements of nature to the residence. Indeed, in a very artificial way: the boundary of the Venus Terrace is defined by box-cut linden trees, the circular cake-like flower beds leave only little room for nature to enfold. In this zone, nature is taking on the forms of architecture – like the conifers nestled up against the building that take up the forms of the conical roofs of the little round towers. Around the Venus Terrace, the crenelated encasing wall brings to mind late medieval depictions of the *hortus conclusus*.

The second zone is the Pleasure Grounds, the perfectly manicured lawn on the palace's eastern side with its graceful groupings of exotic conifers, which are now quite tall. Only the Ulmenallee (Avenue of Elms), between the hill gate and the main entrance runs straight. Footpaths and trails are curved, accentuating the park landscape's relief.

The transition to nature is provided by the hillside lawn sloping down towards the Rhine and followed by the forests with the Felsenmeer (Sea of Rocks). Beyond the property limits, little trees, that at some point seeded themselves, have grown in such a way that they significantly hinder the views from the palace to the Rhine valley – and of course vice versa. An unchanged natural attraction on the western side of the property is the Felsenmeer with its trachyte blocks that are towered in chaotic formations.

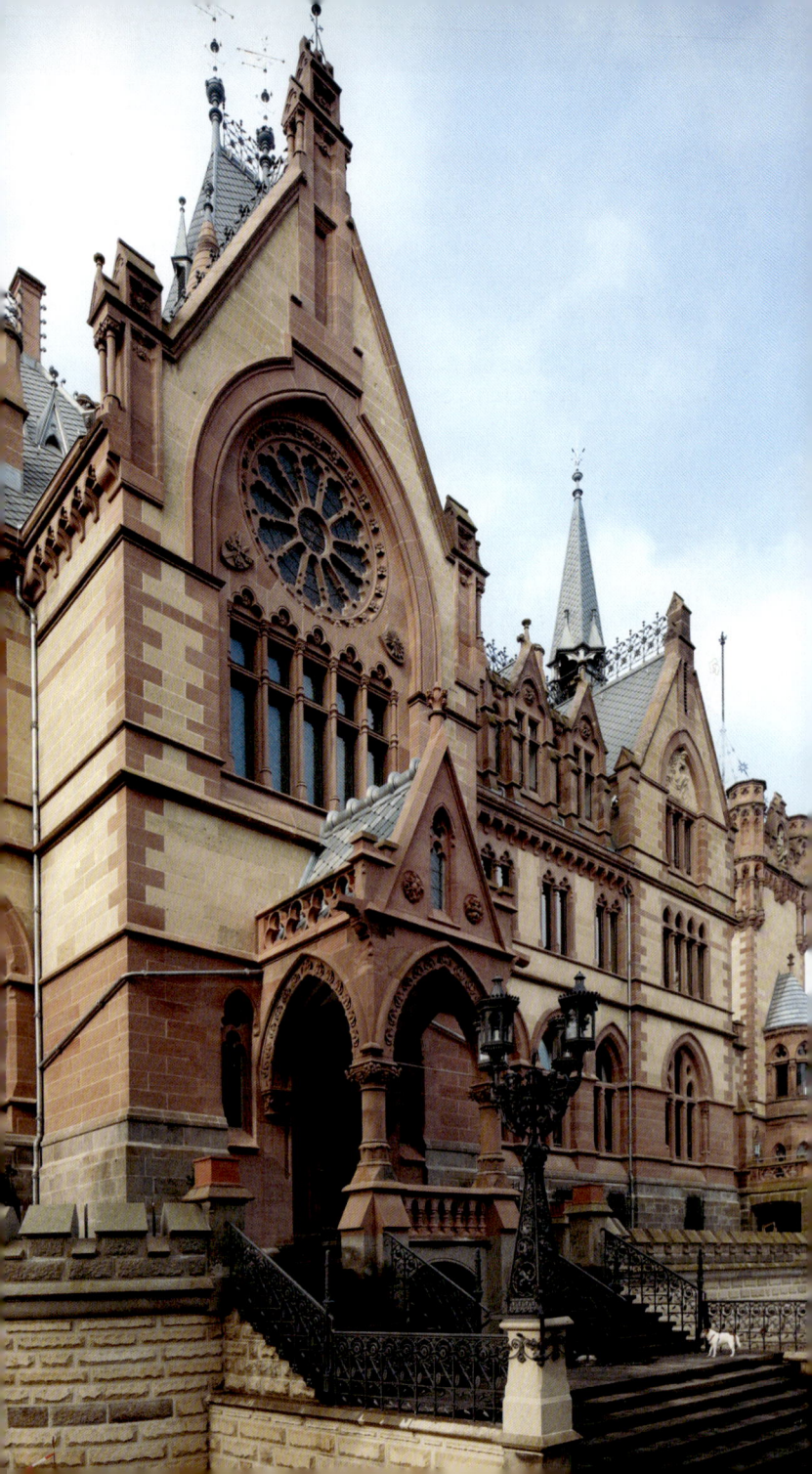

THE PALACE BUILDINGS

To the north on the valley side – on the left – connected to the protrusion accentuating the Reception and Music Halls, is the Main Tower, which towers over everything. It has a protruding ridge with round corner look-outs and a steep hip roof. Between this and the somewhat lower Northern Tower is a stretched out, one-story, structural element on a pedestal. The centre of its façade is accentuated by a gable flanked by little towers and a cupola in the area of the roof. The veneer's continuous red shows: there are no wall surfaces here; everything is structure, décor, or a window.

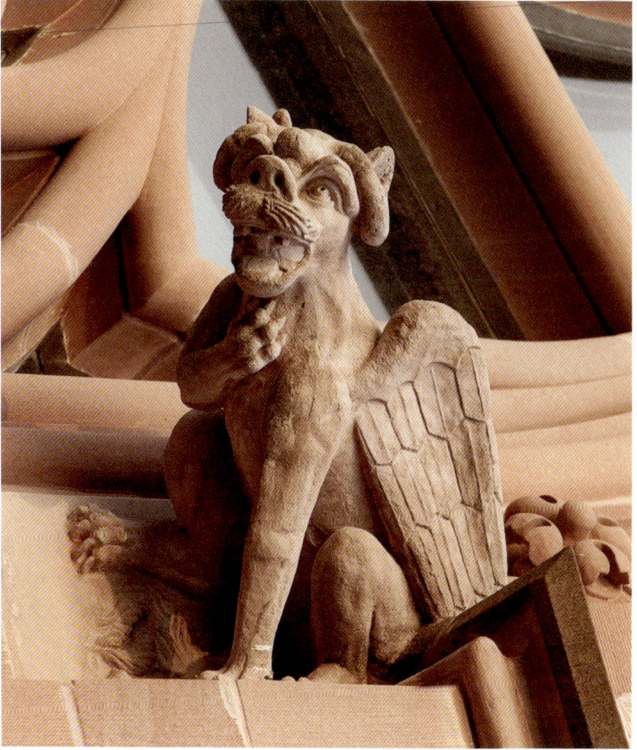

Detail of the exterior in the area of the Art Gallery

View of the entrance area from the southeast

THE PALACE BUILDINGS

The Architectural Sculpture

Schloss Drachenburg displays sculptures on all sides. From capitals, friezes, tracery, and gargoyles, to crests, mottos, and emblems, to deeply meaningful reliefs and figures, the baldachins of which convey a certain sense of the sacred.

The ornamental sculptural architecture recalls models from the thirteenth century, but the precise and meaty execution gives it away as historical decoration without any attempt at dissemblance. The gargoyles leaning far out from the facades are functionless citations from medieval church architecture. Following ancient tradition, they appear as winged monsters (image p. 27).

Crests, mottos, and emblems are concentrated on the northern part of the Drachenburg. As an emblem of the palace complex, the winged dragon rises up from a battlement above the Carriage Hall's portal in the castle's terrace base (image above). On the balcony on the northern side of the Northern Tower,

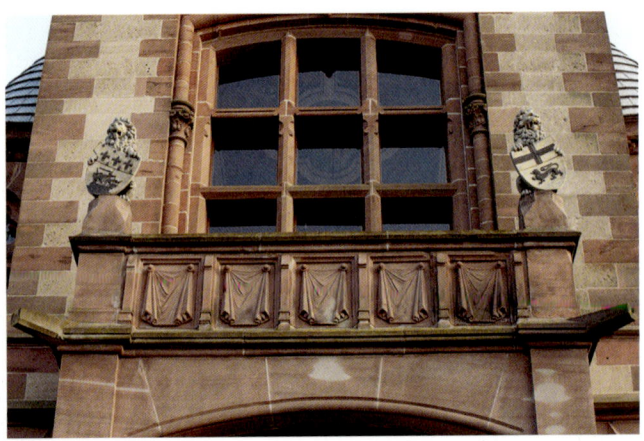

Balcony of the Northern Tower seen from below, inside is the Wedding Chamber, on the left the crest of Paris, on the right that of Bonn

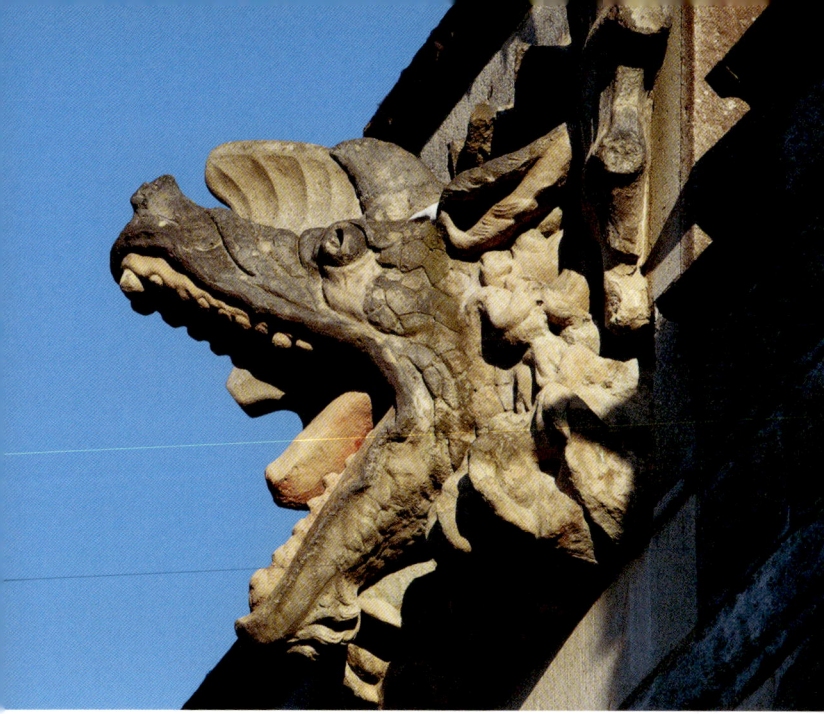

Dragon over the portal of the Carriage Hall

lions present the crests of the cities of Bonn and Paris (image on left): Stephan Sarter was born in one of these cities and enjoyed his successes in the other.

The northern wall of the Northern Towers boasts his crest above this balcony (image p. 30). The split crest shows the dragon to the left, which is also the motif that decorates the helmets, and on the right it displays two crossed canon barrels under a crown.

Above a trefoil arch frieze, the top floor juts out somewhat from the Northern Tower. The corners create polygonal look-outs, which – jutting out further – are supported by columns, on corbels below the friezes. These columns stand separate from the structure. In the middle of each of the crenelated walls between the look-outs are figures seated in raised niches below the stepped gables. On the northern side above the crest sits

THE PALACE BUILDINGS

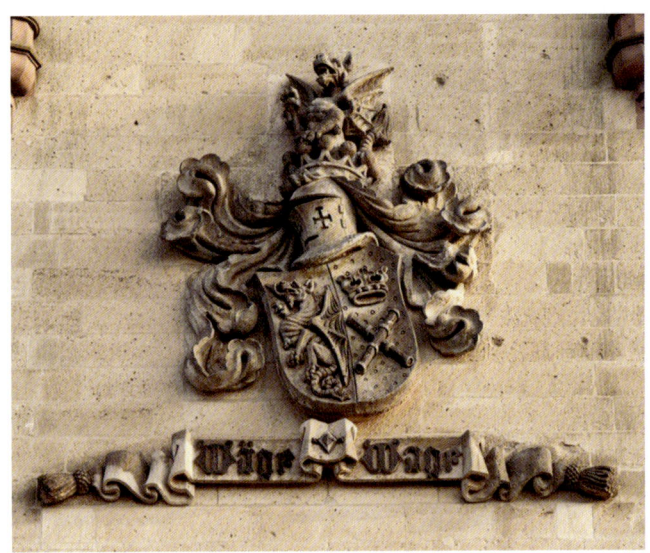

Stephan von Sarter's crest on the Northern Tower

the chief cathedral architect, Gerhard von Rile († around 1271), looking pensively towards his work, the Cologne Cathedral (image on right). At the time of the groundbreaking ceremony for the Gothic cathedral in 1248, Gerhard von Rile was the head of the construction office. He is presumably the creator of the plans according to which the cathedral was built even into the nineteenth century. His appurtenances are a tablet with the construction plan and a chisel in his left hand.

The sculptures on the other three sides display prototypical heroes of medieval and early modern period art. The poet Wolfram von Eschenbach († around 1220) is renowned for his epic poem Parzival, the inspirational source for Richard Wagner's last opera *Parsifal,* first performed in Bayreuth in 1882. His attribute is a harp. The portrait of the bronze caster Peter Vischer († 1529) is inspired by his self-portrait in Nuremburg's St. Sebaldus Shrine, which depicts him wearing working clothes (image on right).

30   *Wilhelm Albermann, sculpture "Gerhard von Rile" on the Northern Tower*

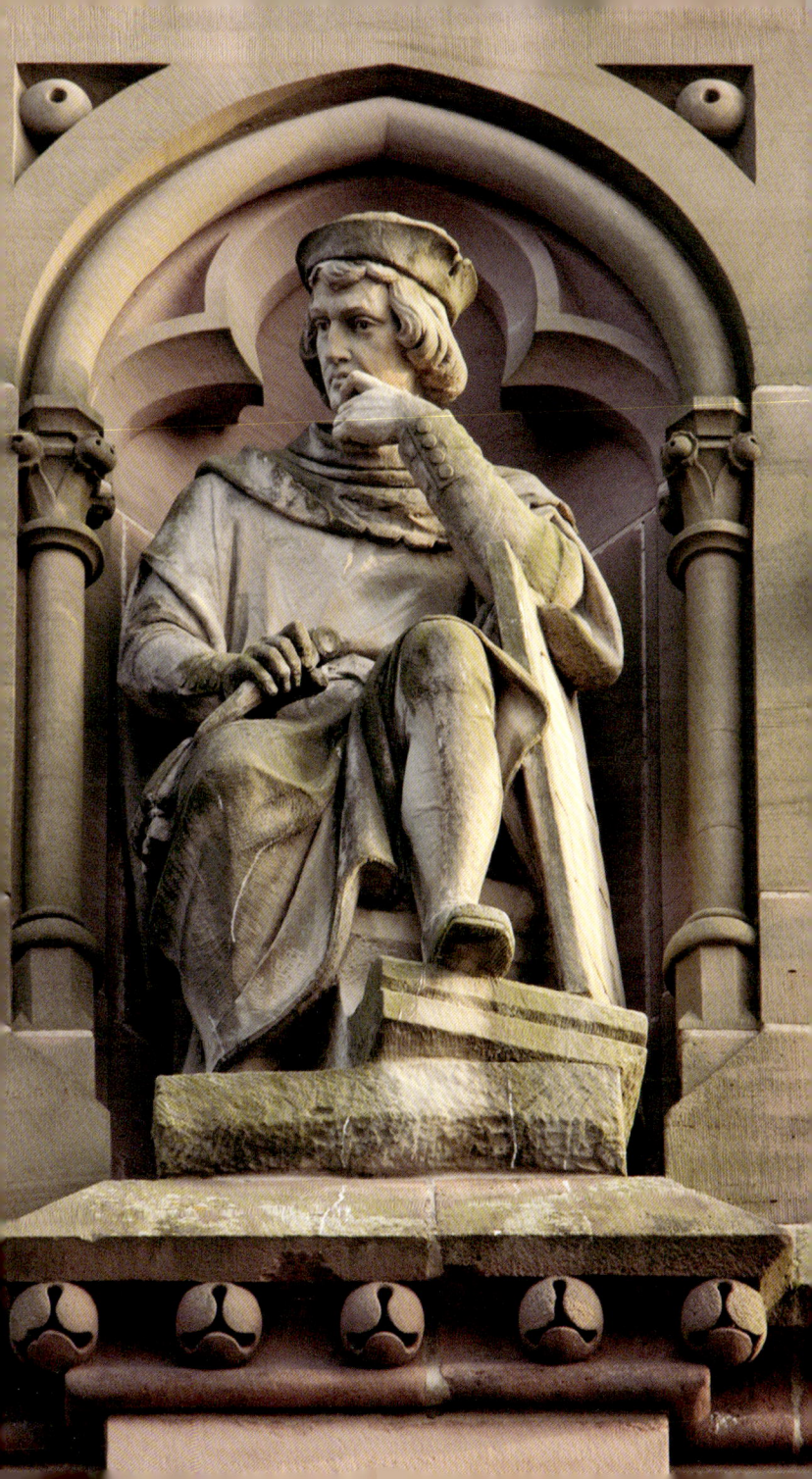

THE PALACE BUILDINGS

Vischer's famous self-portraits were also the basis for the creation of the Albrecht Dürer (1471–1528) figure. The famous painter did not need to be adorned with any further attributes.

The sculptor Wilhelm Albermann (1835–1913) of Cologne created the sculptures. As an independently working sculptor he created countless fountains and war memorials. The "Four Heroes of Art" are an exception in his body of work. Angelika Schyma also attributes the reliefs in the gables of the eastern and western facades to him. They allude to the region's myths: the "Dragon Virgin" (western façade) and the "Lorelei" (image p. 34).

The dragon on the Drachenfels plays a significant role in these myths. One of the topical narrative threads also found elsewhere – like the legend of St. George – describes the dragon as a threatening beast for which virgins must be sacrificed on a set schedule in order to prevent the beast from doing worse things. A hero must appear, to slay the dragon and save the virgin. The dragon that Siegfried killed – Fafnir – was the guard for a treasure, the "Rheingold". As the conqueror of the somewhat harmless appearing lindworm at his feet, Siegfried is displayed on the eastern façade to the left of the main entrance. This is surely symbolic of the appreciation the owner had for Schloss Drachenburg's surroundings (image p. 35).

The stone hero is standing on a polygonal console and above him is a baldachin designed from architectonic motifs. A column stands on the baldachin, supporting a gargoyle that doesn't make much sense in this spot below a dormer. Corbels and baldachins are common motifs for the accentuation of saint depictions in church interiors. In his right arm, which has broken off, Siegfried heaves a sword, a familiar gesture for this able-bodied figure.

The palace's southern façade (image p. 2) has special significance. Together with the Venus Terrace, it creates a beautiful and frequently photographed view from a scenic lookout on the

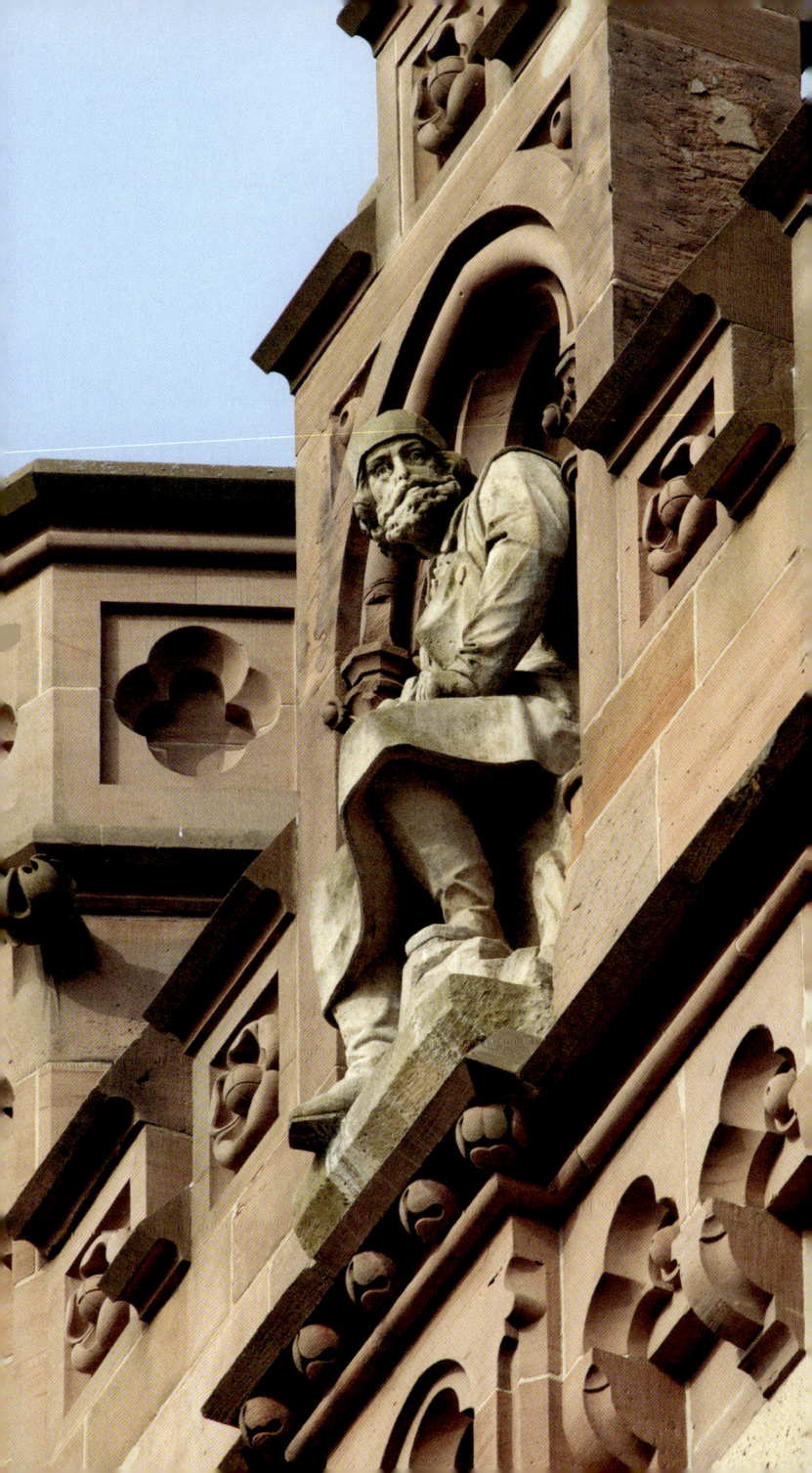

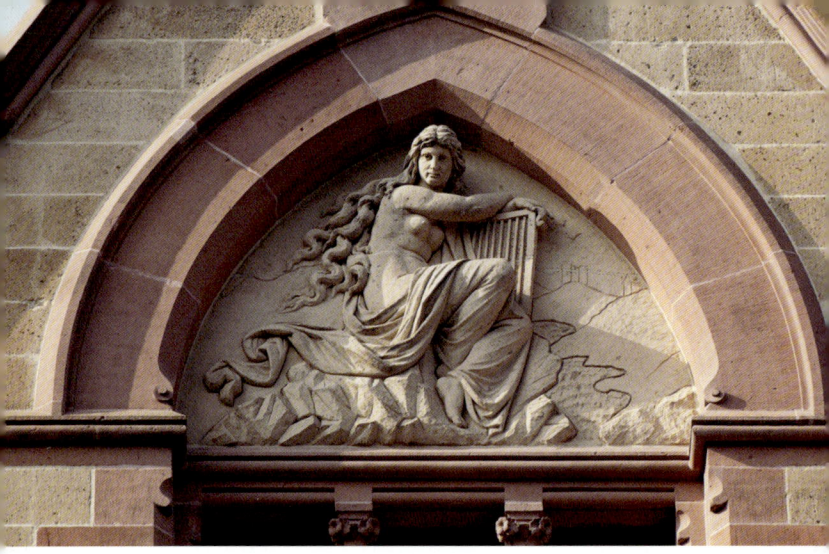

Attributed to Wilhelm Albermann, "Loreley" relief on the eastern gable

path to the Drachenfels. This perspective offers a dazzling variety of architectonic motifs, starting with the garden at the crenelated base of the Venus Terrace, the fountain with the statue of a woman delivered by Paul Spinat, the pedestals with the bronze stags by Pierre Louis Rouillard (1820–1881), and last but not least the boxed linden trees. Next to the three dark arches of a veranda that can be reached from the building only by detours, two bay windows already reveal the grey of the zinc helm roofs in the lower floor. Beautiful asymmetry, especially if the protruding ledges of the eastern façade are included! The upper floor is endowed with nobility by an alcove flanked by statues. In the area of the roofs, this view includes pointed cones and steep pyramids. Above this, there is again a great variety of stones on the Main Tower, the crown of which is made up of stony, red cones and very steep, grey pyramids covered with zinc rhombuses.

The central motif in this wealth of decoration is the oriel window, which on the outside is surrounded by figures heavy with meaning, and on the inside is part of the honorary Guest Room

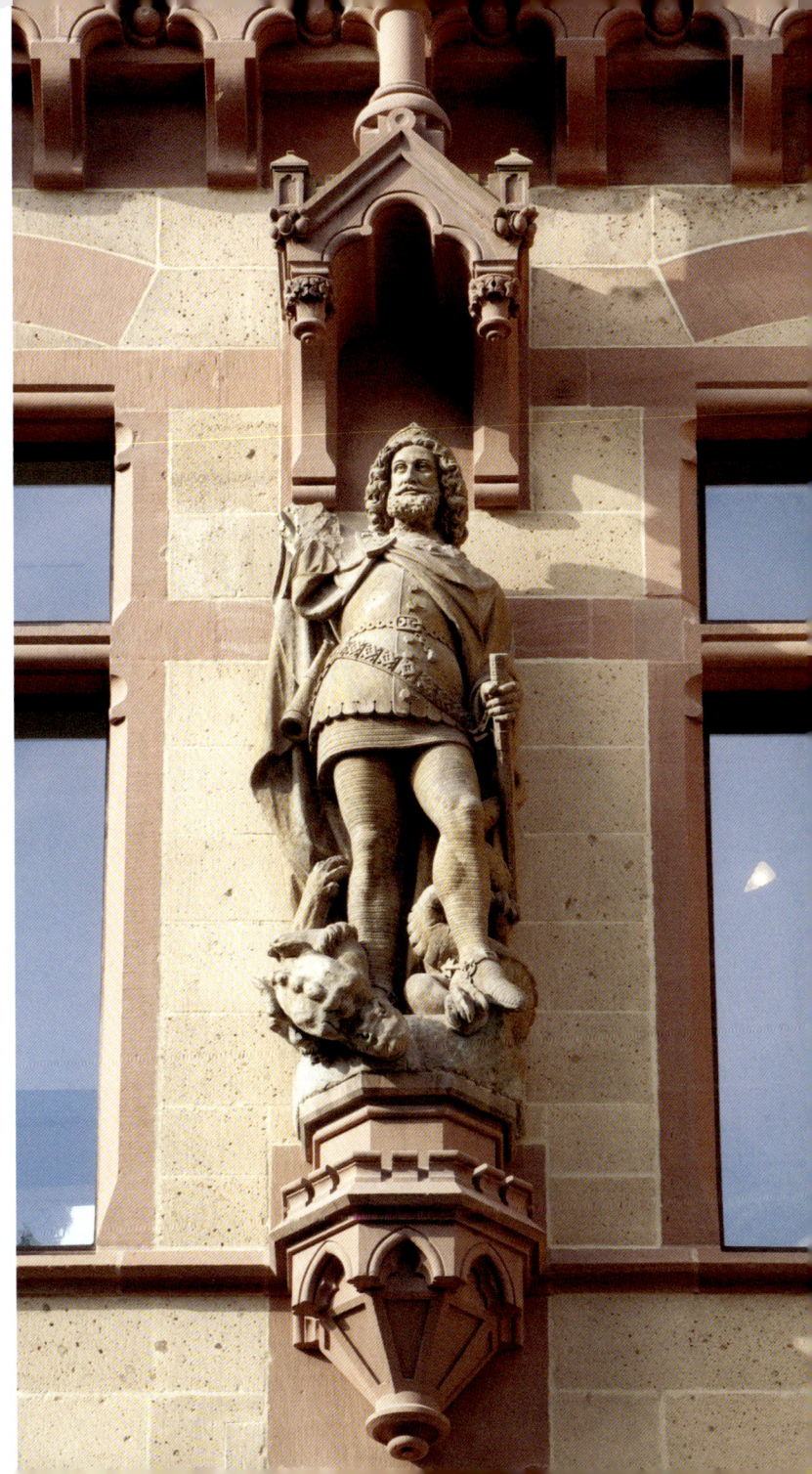

(image on right). The statues, positioned on corbels and under baldachins, depict emperors: In front of the gable, above the conical stone roof of the oriel, stands Julius Caesar, the first emperor of the Roman Empire – as one can read inscribed on the pedestal. Considering the medieval style of his garments, he could hardly be recognized as such without the identification. To the left of the oriel is Charlemagne. The sculpture's design is based on a painting by Albrecht Dürer. The German emperor, Wilhelm I, stands on the corbel to the right. Contemporaries easily recognized him due to his distinctive mutton chops.

With its five-eighths layout, the oriel makes is reminiscent of a small choir of a medieval castle. There are crests attached below the windows, set between cowering corbel gnomes carrying "buttresses". The central crest displays the imperial eagle with the Hohenzollern shield in front of his breast. The right crest shows the Prussian eagle with the sceptre and the *globus cruciger* in its clutches and the initials 'WR' on his chest, for Wilhelmus Rex. On the split shield on the left the imperial eagle and the French fleurs-de-lis are displayed – both nations claim Charlemagne as their empire's founder. The portrait painted in 1513 by Albrecht Dürer shows both the lilies and the eagle on two separate shields.

This combination of the three emperors is one of a kind. However, it mirrors thoughts about legitimation that, for example, led to the construction of the Holy Roman Empire of the German Nation, which based its legitimacy on the Imperium Romanum. In turn, the German Empire, founded in 1871, considered itself to be following in the tradition of the Holy Roman Empire of the German Nation, which had been dissolved in 1806.

The Cologne sculptor Peter Fuchs (1829–1898) signed the sculptures of the three emperors and Siegfried. He had absolved his training in the Cologne cathedral construction workshop. In the course of his professional life, he completed almost 700 sculptures for the cathedral. A statue of Charlemagne that he produced is part of the west façade of the cathedral.

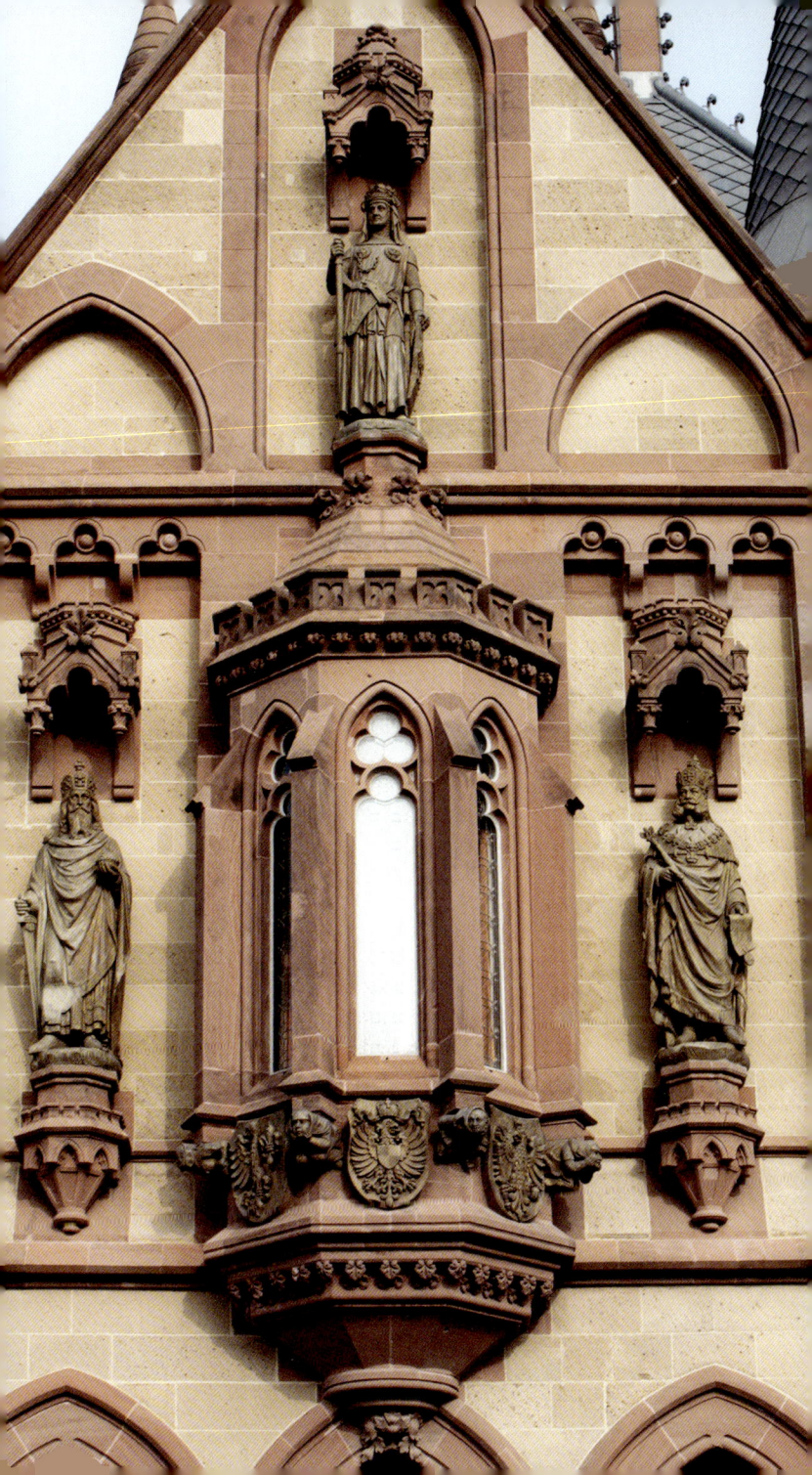

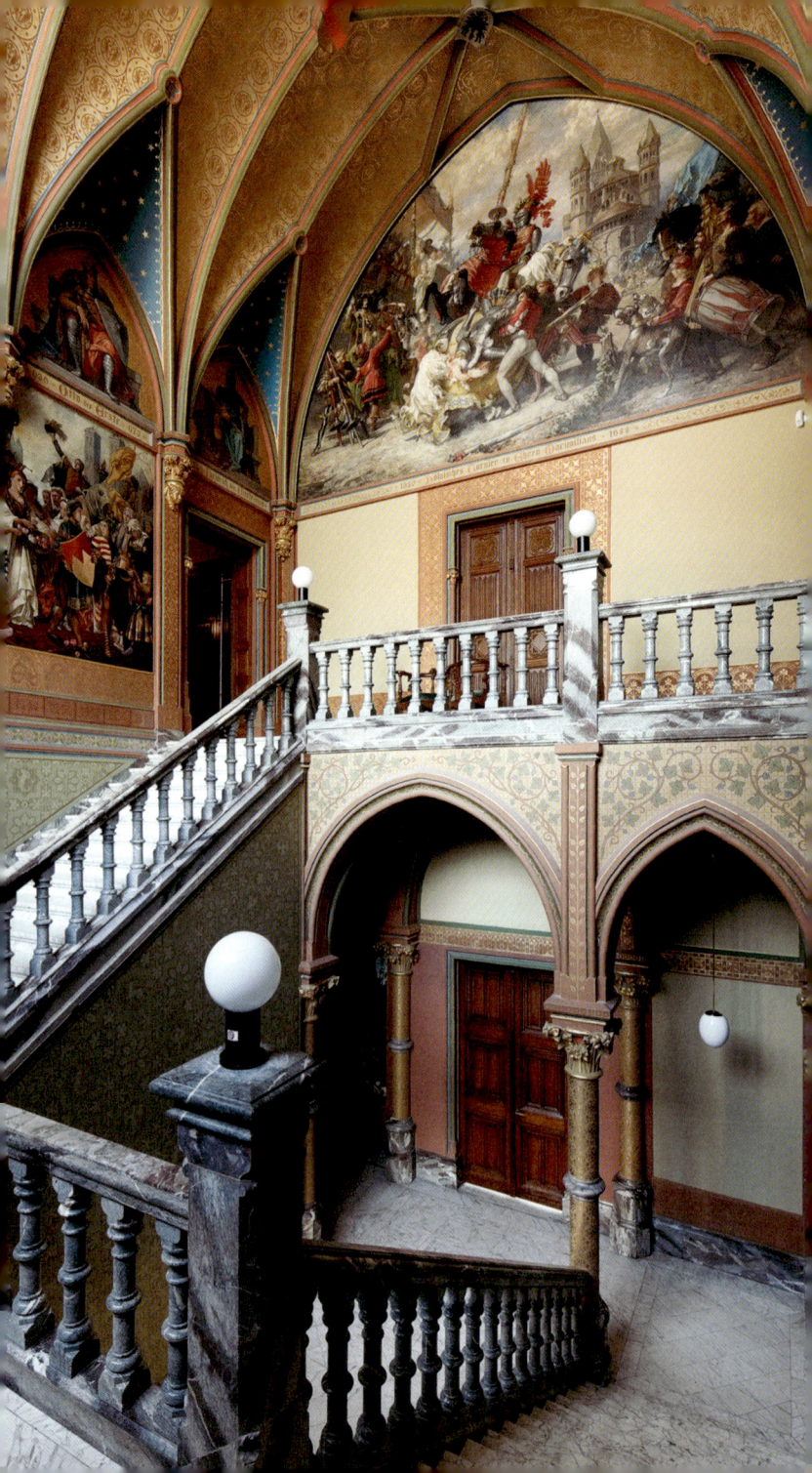

THE INTERIORS

Main Entrance, Vestibule, and Stairwell

After a slight ascent via the Pleasure Grounds, one reaches the main entrance on Schloss Drachenburg's eastern side, which has been restored to its original state. The Vestibule and the Main Stairwell are marked in the façade by a risalit, which juts out quite far, and by a wide outdoor staircase in front of it. A small vaulted porch welcomes the visitor who goes on to reach the stairwell by way of the Vestibule.

The generous complex, the stencilled paintings on the walls and on the architectural elements, the precious materials, large murals, ribbed vaulting, and a stained glass window with a tracery rosette in the eastern wall all combine to create a stately atmosphere. And today what we see is only part of the original splendour. Some of the wall paintings have been lost, others restored and supplemented. The large window, however, is the only stained glass window in the whole castle which has been completely preserved (image p. 40). The eagle at the centre of the rosette is the imperial eagle with the Hohenzollern crest. The same variation of the official imperial eagle can be seen on the oriel in the southern façade.

Especially in the lower areas, there have been irreparable losses in the paintings. One of these is recalled by a postcard photo with a depiction of the Snow White and the Seven Dwarves, a lost painting by Joseph Flüggen (1842–1906), blown up to its original size. In the lunettes above the doors, there were allegorical depictions of the Rhine and its tributaries: of these paintings useable visuals sources no longer even exist.

The river allegories were representative of the owner's close bond to the region, which is expressed in many further details. Thus, the large history paintings in the Main Stairwell depict

Main Stairwell

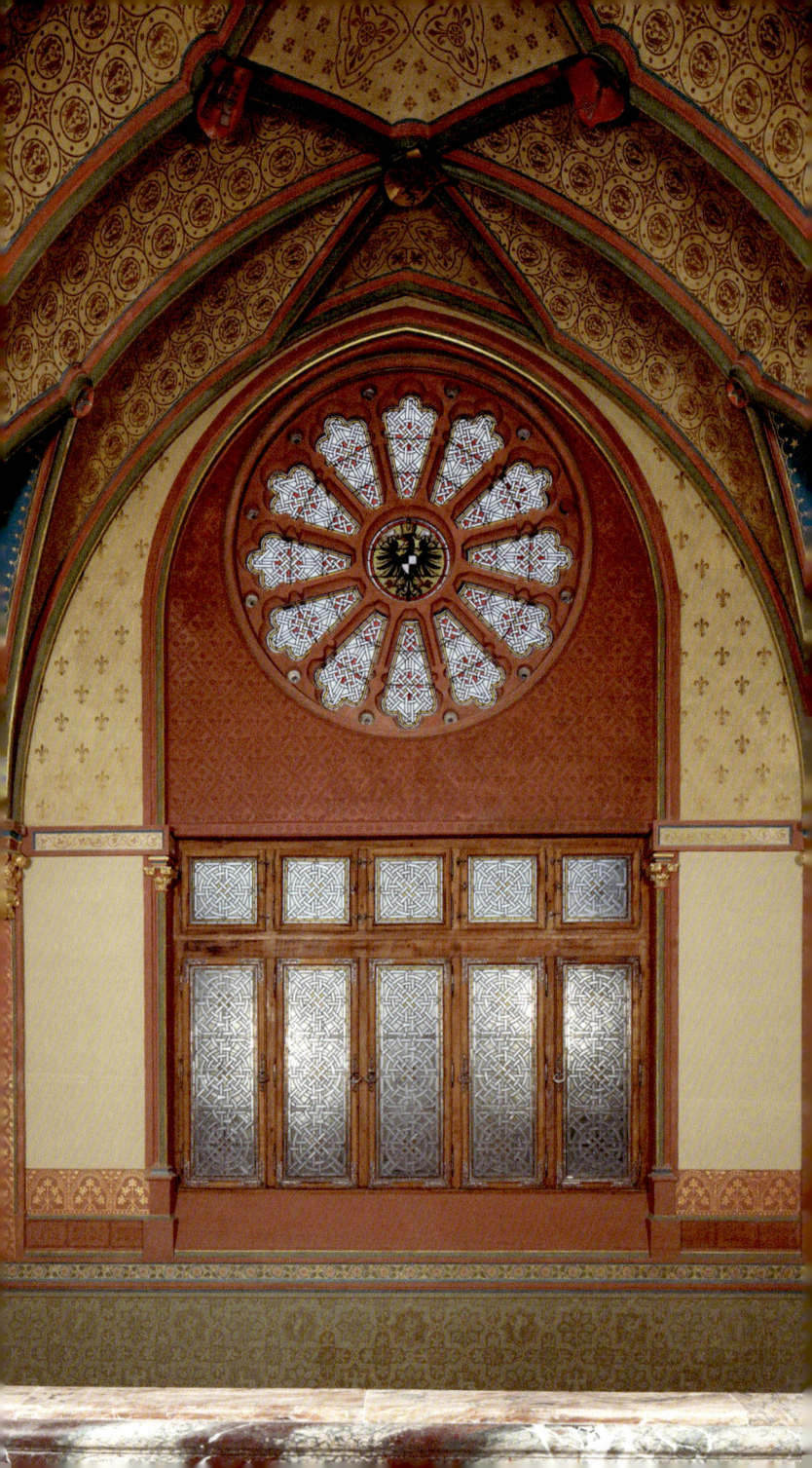

THE INTERIORS

events from German history that took place in Stephan von Sarter's Rhenish homeland. The cornerstone for the Gothic construction of the Cologne Cathedral starting in 1248 was quarried in the "Domkaule" (cathedral pit) at Drachenfels. The wide-format painting by Friedrich von Keller (1840–1914), to the left above the lower part of the stairs, depicts the transport of the stone from Drachenfels to Cologne in a festive procession (image p. 42). An even earlier event is portrayed in the same painter's vertically formatted painting on the same wall to its right. The encounter between the French King Charles III and the German King Henry I ("Henry the Fowler") took place on a ship in the middle of the Rhine near Bonn in order avoid diplomatic problems regarding rank.

Munich Painters in the Rhineland

Schloss Drachenburg was intended to be endowed with comprehensive mural cycles. The painters associated with Düsseldorf's Art Academy were the closest available. Occupied with more than enough commissions, the popular landscape and history painters from Düsseldorf had to decline. As a result, the artists connected to the prestigious Royal Academy of Fine Arts in Munich were the next choice. Before delivering their works for the Drachenburg to the Rhineland, they exhibited them in several exhibitions in Munich and garnered much attention. The discussions of the exhibits in Munich's press are full of accolades and also include the man who commissioned them in their praise.

The technique of marouflage made it possible to exhibit mural painting far from their destination. The painters painted on canvases in Munich, the sizes of which were determined by their ultimate placements. Architect Wilhelm Hoffmann was presumably responsible for the logistics of the procedure in the second phase of planning. The canvas paintings were transportable and thus could be presented in exhibitions, until they arrived in the Rhineland and were attached to the walls or arch surfaces for which they were intended. As a result, this construction project in Königswinter also received attention in the southern German metropolis of Munich.

Window in the east wall of the Main Stairwell

THE INTERIORS

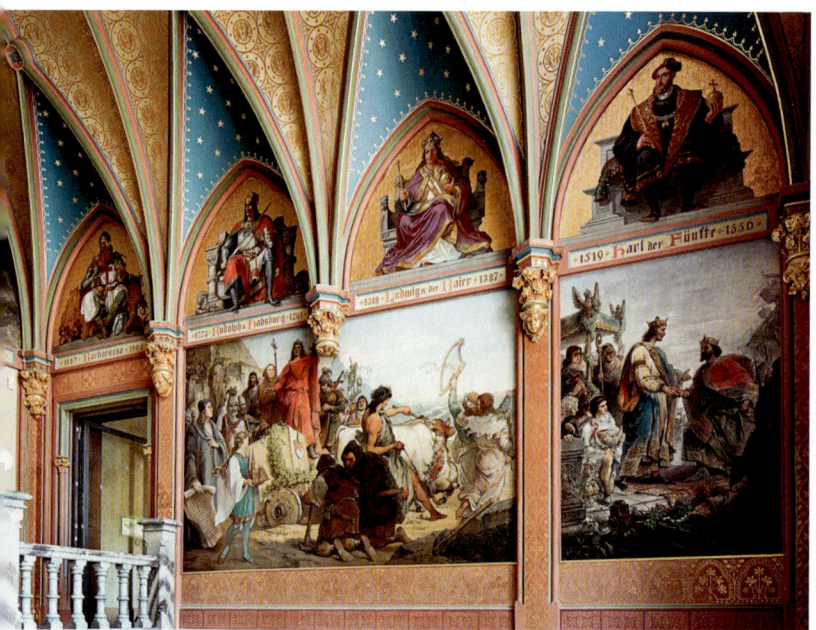

Northern wall of the Main Stairwell with paintings by Friedrich von Keller

The opposite wall along the upper portion of the stairs, at the height of the pedestal, boasts the painting Sängerkrieg auf der Insel Nonnenwerth 1338 vor dem englischen König Eduard III by Heinrich Heim (1850–1921). The scenes in which these episodes took place are in visual range of the Drachenburg. Heinrich Heim also painted the following scene, the location of which can be determined by the view of the towers flanking the choir of St. Gereon in Cologne (image p. 43). A patrician from Cologne is said to have married a British prince's daughter in 1201. The scene of the tournament on the wall opposite the tracery rosette was painted by Carl Rickelt (1857–1919) (image p. 44). On the occasion of the imperial diet in Cologne in 1505, "the last knight", Holy Roman Emperor Maximilian I (1459–1519) was honoured with a tournament. Cologne's Neumarkt is clearly recognizable

THE INTERIORS

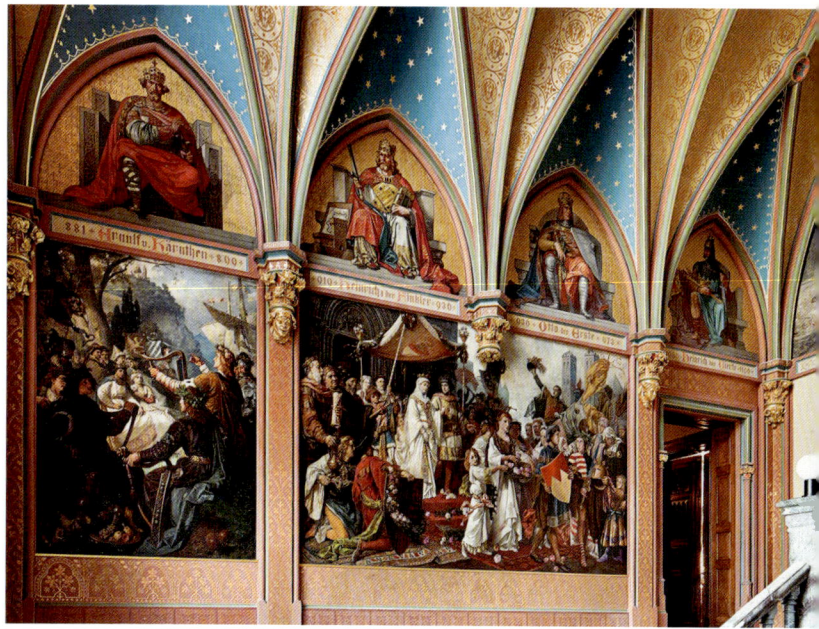

Southern wall of the Main Stairwell with paintings by Heinrich Heim

as the location of the jousting lane due to the choir of the Basilica of the Holy Apostles.

In the lunettes above the history paintings, Heinrich Flüggen painted the idealized portraits of enthroned German kings and emperors. The criteria for the selection, out of a long line of monarchs of the Holy Roman Empire of the German Nation, are not always clear. But in any case, combined with a version of the crest of Second German Empire (1871–1918) modified in favour of the House of Hohenzollern, they represent von Sarter's allegiance to the state.

The staging of the arrival is focused on the wall across from the entry portal, i.e. on the second floor (Level 5), the window. On

THE INTERIORS

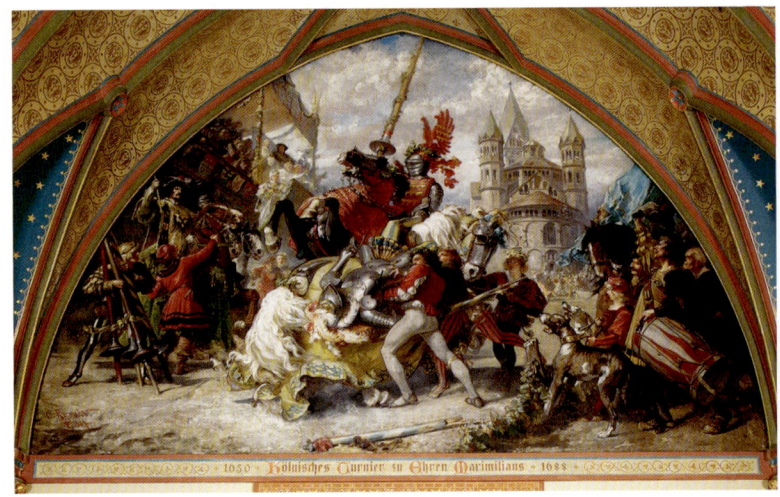

Carl Rickelt, "Tournament at Cologne's Neumarkt"

the lower, representative floor (Level 4), the visitor proceeds straight to the door leading to the Reception Hall – from which point other representative rooms follow. But there are also side routes. A visitor turning to the right reaches a tight, narrow side stairwell that connects to the Main Tower. A left turn leads to the hunting and breakfast room – a small room with three-bay cross-ribbed vaulting (right image). This room was intended to be the gathering area for hunting parties leaving early in the morning. The door panels in the historic serving cabinet made of light oak display mythical creatures and strap work motifs that had been widely circulated by German lesser masters during the sixteenth century to inspire the craftspeople of the time and which again became popular in the nineteenth century. The furniture, chandeliers, and even the antlers have been purchased since the 1990s, like most of the transportable interior décor.

The wainscoting that takes up the lower third of the wall space, on the other hand, has survived mostly in its original condition.

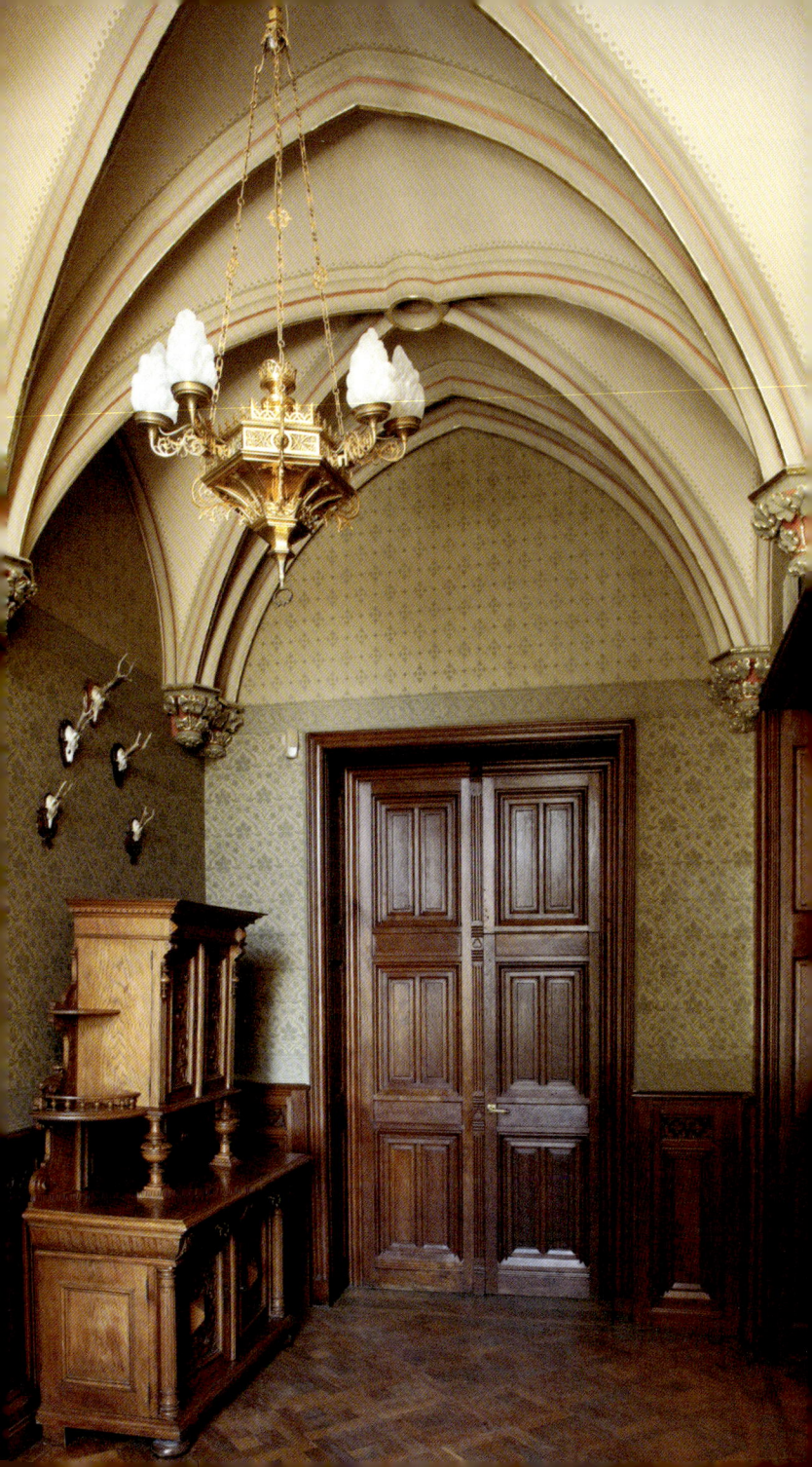

THE INTERIORS

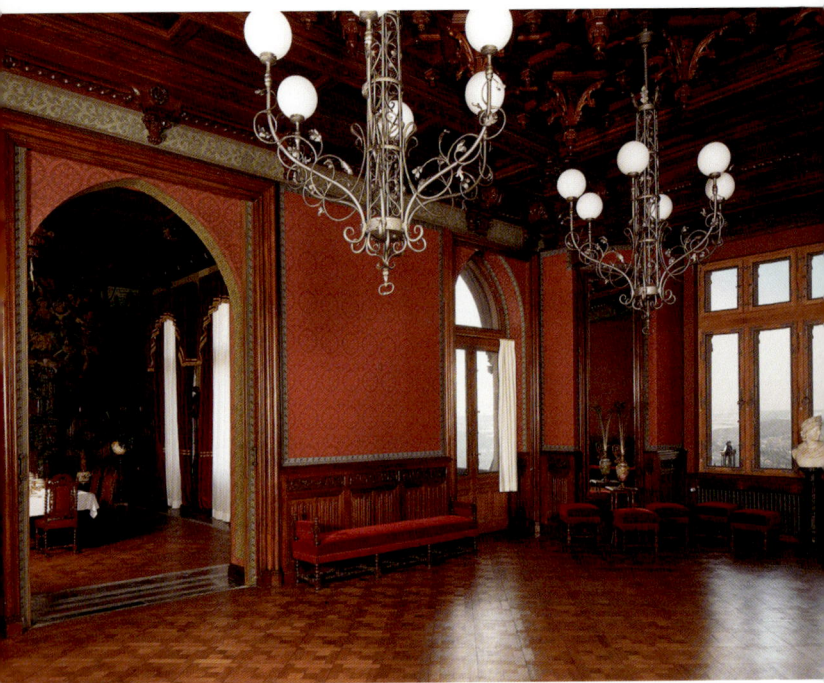

Reception Hall

The ornamental decoration with stencilled paintings has been reconstructed based on on-site findings. There are "windows" in many parts of the Drachenburg that bear "witness" to these findings: through meticulous work, the original wall decorations have been revealed below many layers of paint. Observant visitors will not fail to notice this documentation of the original state of the palace.

Reception Hall

From the Main Stairwell, the visitor is led into the Reception Hall (left image). It is not only the size of the room that impresses those entering. Above a panelled base with folded plate decor, the wall is decorated with pomegranate motifs in a Bordeaux-red repetitive pattern. The beams under the ceiling and the narrow frame offer a contrast in tones of green. Above, the wooden coffered ceiling is truly opulent and highly detailed. Its mahogany tone is in harmony with the walls. The head builder Franz Langenberg (1842–1895) contributed the designs. Wide frames and panels attached very low define the ceiling construction, its three-dimensionality accentuated by elements that hang deep into the room. The candelabras hanging from the ceiling are reconstructions based on old photos of the room.

The bust of the ancient Greek god of the arts, Apollo, belongs to the original interior design and luckily could be repurchased. Its prominent placement in the Reception Hall is confirmed by old photos and was intended to highlight von Sarter's self-presentation as a patron of the arts. Today, four paintings by the Düsseldorf painter Christian Eduard Boettcher (1818–1889) hang on the walls and depict landscapes from the Rhine Gorge.

The Reception Hall is true to its name, providing access to the opulent hall for festive banquettes on the one side, and a series of rooms with varying layouts to the other, which tend to the various needs of guests at large festivities. There are also two balconies that can be accessed from the Reception Hall. One of these is connected to the western terrace by a curved staircase.

THE INTERIORS

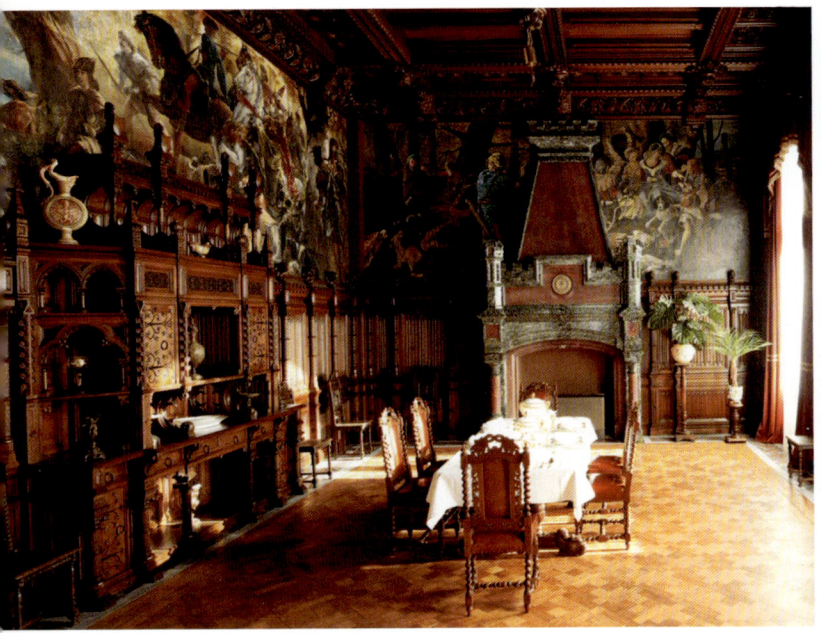

Dining Room

Dining Room

In massive opulence of interior decor, the Reception Hall is even outdone by the Dining Room (image above). The wooden ceiling is defined by a deep relief pattern. Additionally, beams and panels are decorated with detailed carvings. The wainscoting reaches up to almost half the height of the room here and is constructed as a frame with panels. Columns on high pedestals accentuate the height. The studs above this extend across the wide, closing cornice. Most of the wood is decorated with carvings, while the upper panels show how the late medieval folded plate motif can be carried even further. As a part of the wainscoting, and accommodating it in size, a richly decorated and finely worked buffet in the centre of the

THE INTERIORS

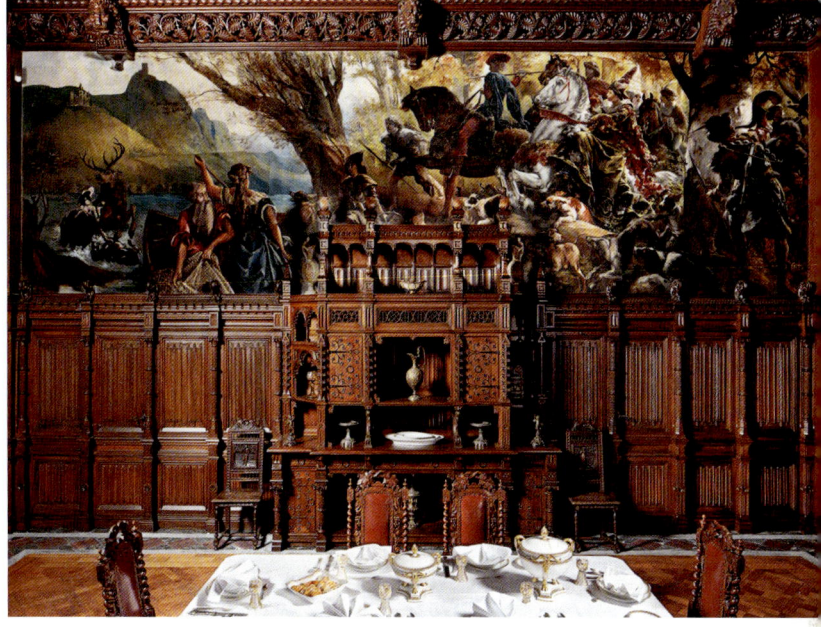

Dining Room, east wall

eastern wall has survived (image above). The alternating open and closed compartments are interesting – the open areas provide space to display valuable pieces of decorative art from the second half of the nineteenth century. The closed areas have glue-laminated panels and as such were not taking advantage of the newest technology available in the nineteenth century. But in this way, they provided the artist blacksmith with an opportunity to transform the hinges into lavish ornamentation. The fireplace made out of contrasting red and green stone is also part of the original interior. From the beginning, the villa was equipped with central heating and the fireplace was for aesthetic purposes only. Franz Langenberg created the designs; the Rümann Company in Hanover did the execution of the woodwork.

THE INTERIORS

Between the wooden panelling of the ceiling and walls, murals with hunting motifs offer an idealized panorama of the area surrounding the Drachenfels. Ferdinand Wagner (1847–1927) from Munich created the depiction of the hunt. Of his paintings, only the area on the eastern wall to the right of the sideboard has been preserved. The other areas are more or less faithful reproductions of his paintings – unfortunately also the stag hunt with the Drachenfels and the Drachenburg in the background, on the left next to the sideboard.

Recognizable Places in the Murals

The painting on the east wall of the Dining Room, in which the castle deviates strongly from its actual appearance – in the northern part, in the area of the Art Gallery and the Northern Tower – is sadly only a reconstruction of the original painting by Ferdinand Wagner. If this depiction of Schloss Drachenburg were authentic, it would possibly offer arguments for its construction history, specifically, regarding the change from the Düsseldorf construction company Tüshaus & von Abbema to architect Wilhelm Hoffmann working in Paris.

In other parts of the picture, the references to specific locations are obvious, and also preserved in the form intended in the nineteenth century. The city of Cologne is clearly identifiable by St. Gereon's choir towers and the choir of the Basilica of the Holy Apostles at the Neumarkt. The murals depicting it are in the Main Stairwell. The Worms Cathedral, in connection to the Siegfried saga – portrayed in the Nibelung Room – is also easily discernible due to its distinctive western towers.

It is apparent that the painters in Munich had the assignment to ensure the identifiability of some locations with the help of distinctive features. But the references are limited to single features. The surroundings of the Worms Cathedral's southern portal have little in common with the open staircase that is portrayed in the picture. The Neumarkt in Cologne is vague and a church portal with this view of St. Gereon does not exist.

THE INTERIORS

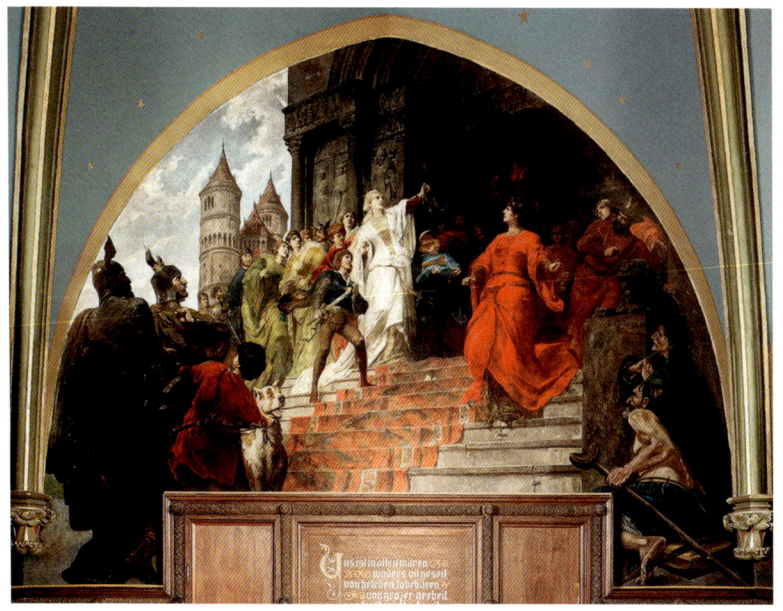

Frank Kirchbach, the struggle between Kriemhild and Brunhild on the steps of the Worms Cathedral

Nibelung Room

The small room north of the adjacent Reception Hall is called the Nibelung Room on account of its wall murals. The painter Frank Kirchbach (1859 -1912) from Munich faced the challenge of difficult formats: on three of the four walls terminating in pointed arches only side strips remain surrounding the ogival openings of a window and two doors. The painter was adept at making use of these limitations to create tall compositions, thus heightening the drama. Even on the full area of the fourth wall, the motif of the stairs presents the opportunity to depict the two battling women, Kriemhild and Brunhild, on the steps of the Worms Cathedral from a dramatic, low-angle perspective (image above). Intent on carrying out an

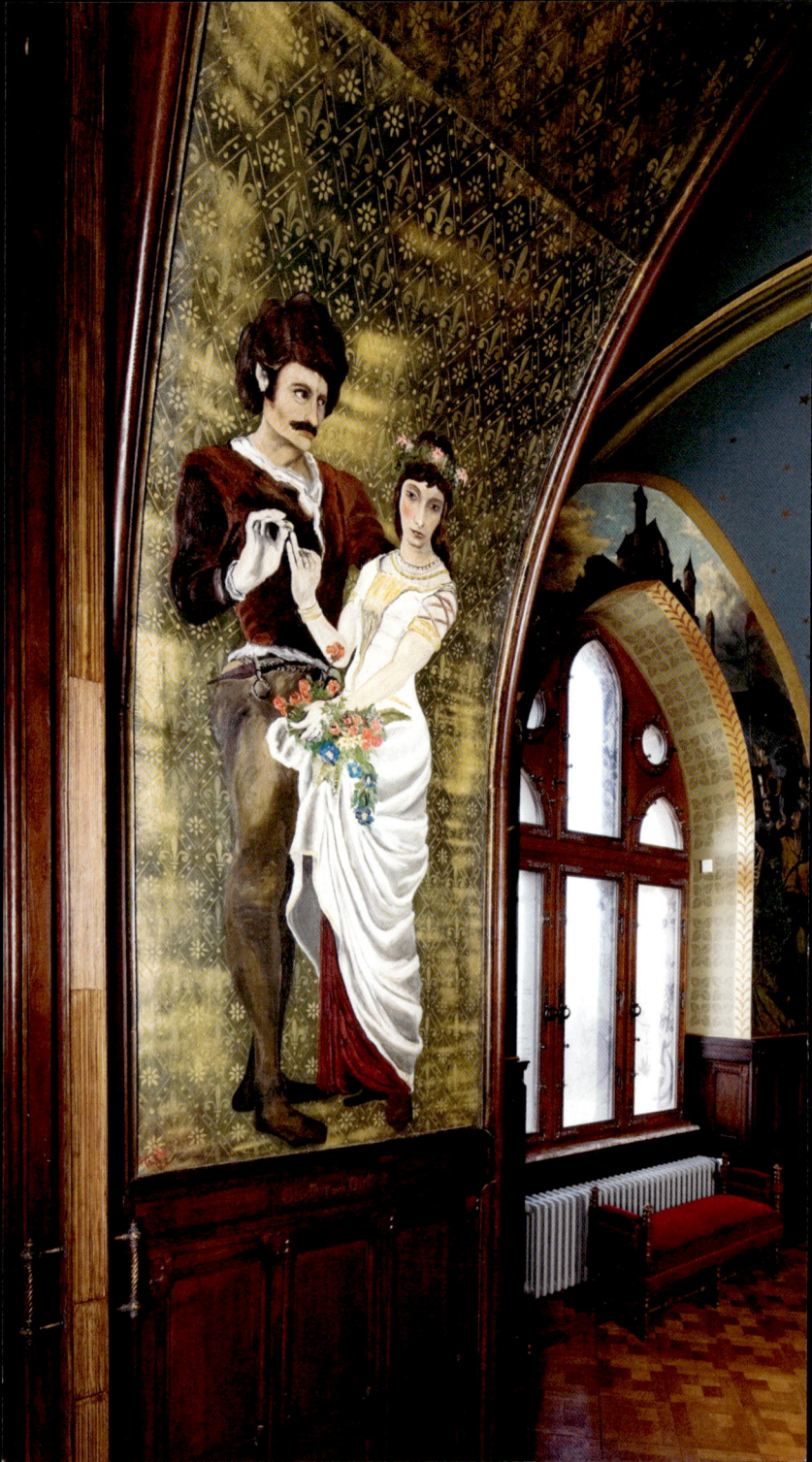

THE INTERIORS

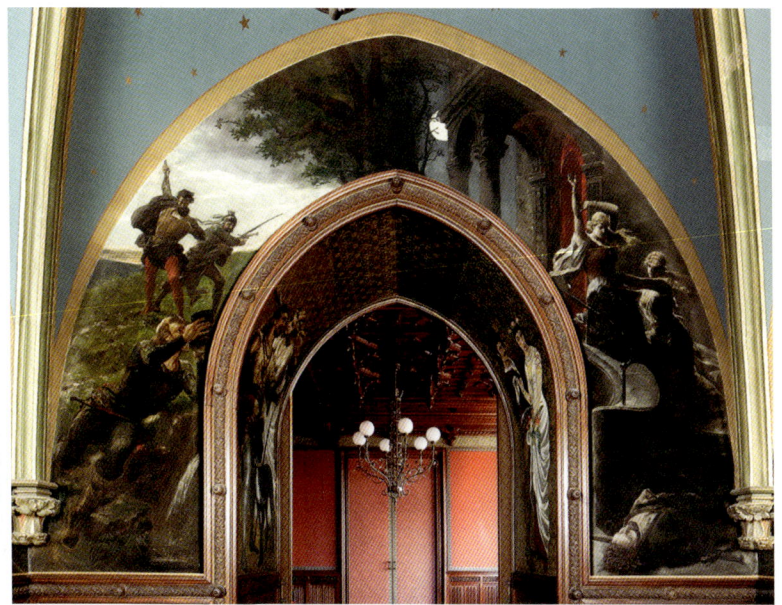

Frank Kirchbach, Siegfried with the moon, and the discovery of his corpse

ignominious murder, Hagen von Tronje slyly creeps over a hill, approaching Siegfried lying by a spring in the foreground. On the other side of the door to the Reception Hall, Kriemhild discovers Siegfried's lifeless body at the foot of a staircase (image above). On the way to the castle of Margrave Rüdiger von Bechelaren the travellers must proceed uphill, the castle is located above the window. On the wall surrounding the northern door, revenge is the motif: Hagen has been captured and Kriemhild decapitates him. She herself is then murdered by Hildebrand at the bottom of a staircase, down which fall the Burgundians, slaughtered further above at the court of Etzel.

The scene with fighting women is signed on the bottom left by Frank Kirchbach. His signature is no longer complete; the

Peter Tutzauer, Gieselher and Dietlind

painting was badly damaged and had to be partly reconstructed. The paintings of pairs from the Nibelung saga, whose names are included in the panels below in archaic forms, are completely new. These were signed in 1972 by the painter Peter Tutzauer and dated: "Tutz 72". And indeed, Giselher can be identified as a child of the 70s by his sideburns (image p. 52).

The three-part window on the western side had stained glass until its destruction. The climbing roses and the battle between the eagles and the domesticated falcons were also designed by Frank Kirchbach. His sketches are preserved at the Franz Mayer'sche Hofkunstanstalt (Franz Mayer of Munich, Inc.) in Munich and served as the basis for the sketchy depiction seen in the window today. As an allusion to Kriemhild's dream, in which two eagles killed her hunting falcon, the stained glass painting was part of the iconographic theme in the Nibelung Room.

Art Gallery

Leaving the Nibelung Room to the north, one passes through a smaller room, which nevertheless feels quite noble due to its vaulting, into the Art Gallery. This is a long, stretched room with coffered barrel vaulting and an ogival profile (right image). The centre between the three bays on each side is covered with a star vault and accentuated by wide, high, tracery windows on the east and the west. The western side of the room dissolves completely into windows, while on the eastern side this is only the case for the northern section

Two sections in one of the windows on the western side show what affect the bright room, flooded with light, would have had. Stained glass was intended for all of the windows and was executed by the Mayer'schen Hofkunstanstalt according to plans by the architect Wilhelm Hofmann.

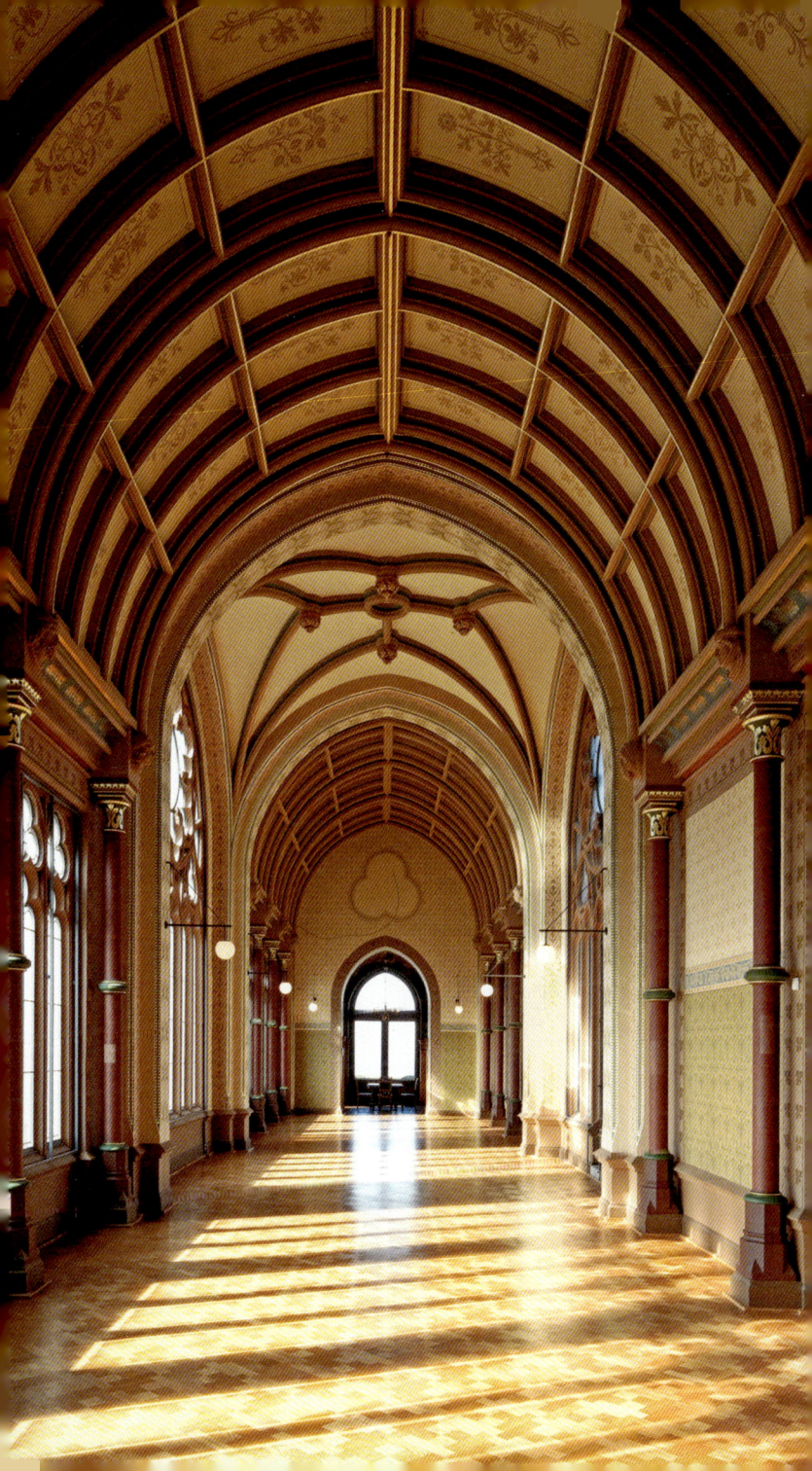

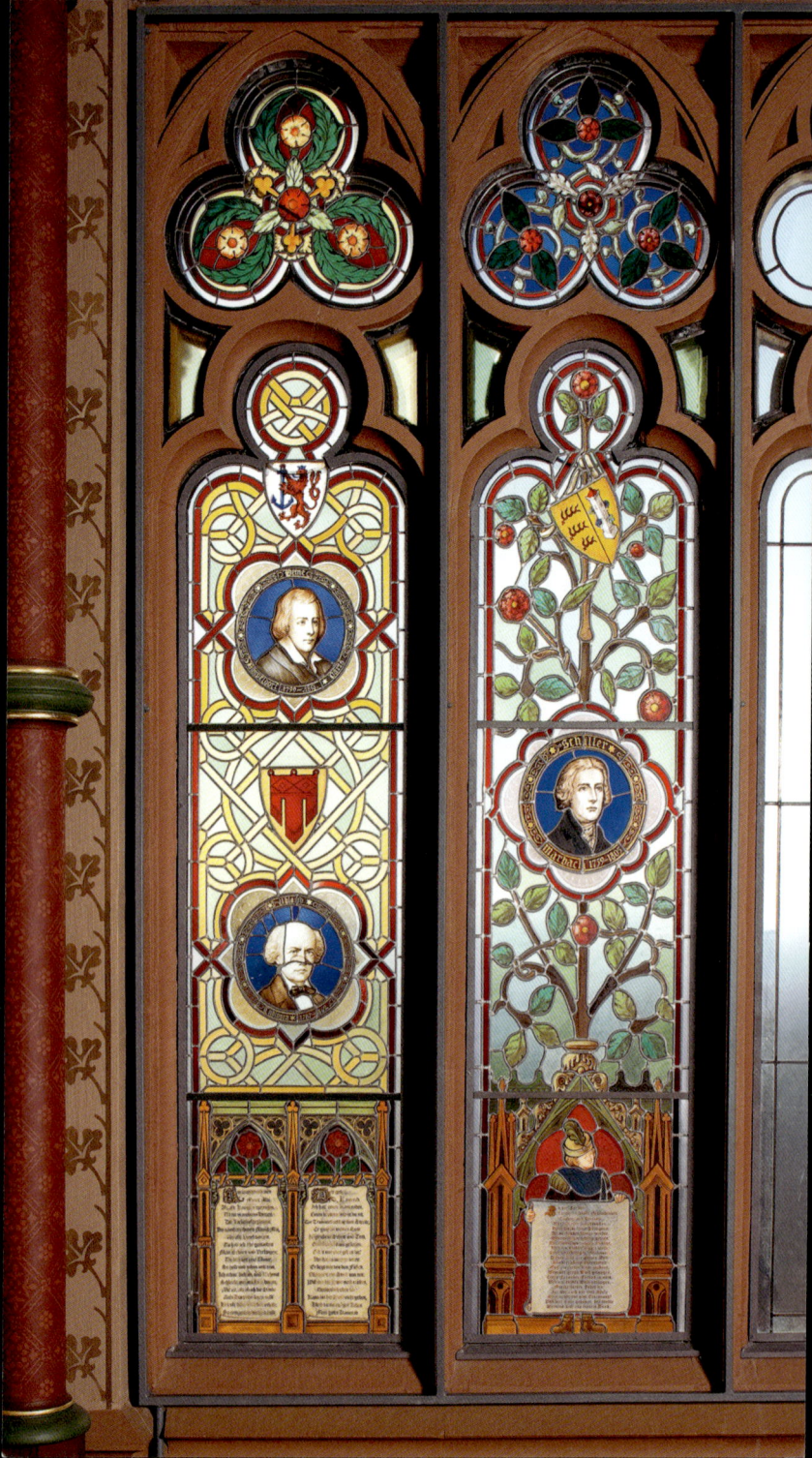

THE INTERIORS

The iconographic theme resulted in an assembly of famous personalities from art, culture, and history and, as such, once again displayed von Sarter's universal education. If the Drachenburg seemed like the "Neuschwanstein of the Rhineland", then the Art Gallery was seen by contemporaries as the "Valhalla of the Rhineland". Carefully organized by category, politicians, musicians, poets, painters, sculptors and builders, queens and empresses, as well as inventors and explorers were portrayed in full figure or as busts in medallions.

The stained glass was destroyed in the Second World War. In 2003, however, a medallion with the bust of the poet Ludwig Uhland was purchased; it could be identified as a fragment of the great series (left image). The Mayer'sche Hofkunstanstalt, the stained-glass studio that is flourishing to this day, reconstructed the window around the medallion according to the plans from its archive. Besides the medallion with Uhland's portrait, there is also one further one portraying Heinrich Heine. Each poet is also supplemented with the crest of their hometown: Düsseldorf for Heine and Tübingen for Uhland. Below, there is a poem by each of the poets. The "Ernst and Anna Reimann and Eduard and Ursula Reimann Foundation" is responsible for the complete reconstruction of the Schiller window on the right.

But it still takes a good amount of imagination to visualize the tall room bathed fully in the coloured light of the original stained glass series. Together with the vaults, the light must have created an impression of sacredness. During the time in which the Christian Brothers were running the boarding school, St. Michael's (1930–1940), the Art Gallery was arranged for use as a chapel and the adjacent drinking salon was the adjoining sacristy.

Two reconstructed windows in the Art Gallery with the original portrait of Ludwig Uhland

THE INTERIORS

Tavern Room

The drinking salon, or Tavern Room, is all about wine, women, and song, as can be seen clearly in the paintings by Herman Schneider (1847–1918) with their bacchanalian scenes (right image). Of course, while the room was being used as a sacristy in the 1930s, the unclothed men, women, and children were painted over. It was not until the 1970s that the owner at the time, Paul Spinat, had the vault paintings uncovered and recreated according to old photos (image p. 60/61).

The classic themes – Bacchus, Ariadne, Nymphs, and much more – offer the pretence of satisfying male fantasies. The small chamber provides the option to retreat from the Art Gallery, perhaps in order to take part in conversations between men over a glass or two of wine.

The room on the bottom floor of the Northern Tower opens up westwards with an oriel offering views of the Rhine. In good weather, a balcony accessible through the northern door allows a view of the distinctive silhouette of the Cologne Cathedral on the horizon. The eastern door opens to a staircase tower that leads to a wedding chamber one story higher, which, together with the gastronomic offerings in the Front Building, provides the prerequisites for beautiful weddings in a magnificent ambience.

Modern steel stairways make accessible two further floors in the Northern Tower, offering the complete panorama: Cologne to the north, Bonn and Bad Godesberg to the northwest, the Eifel to the west, Rolandseck, the island Nonnenwerth, and the Drachenfels to the south, the Siebengebirge to the east, and the Petersberg in the northeast.

Tavern Room, view to the west

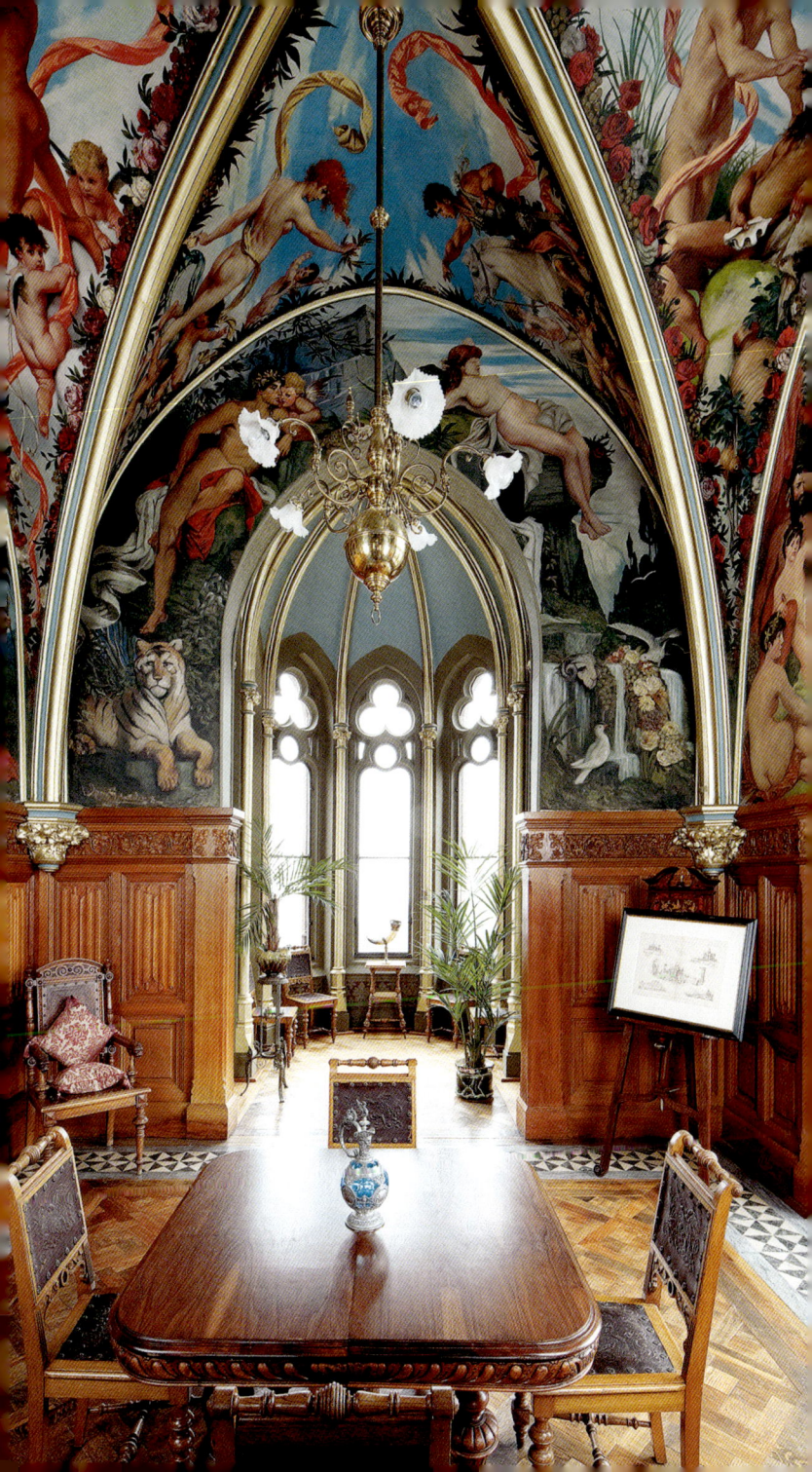

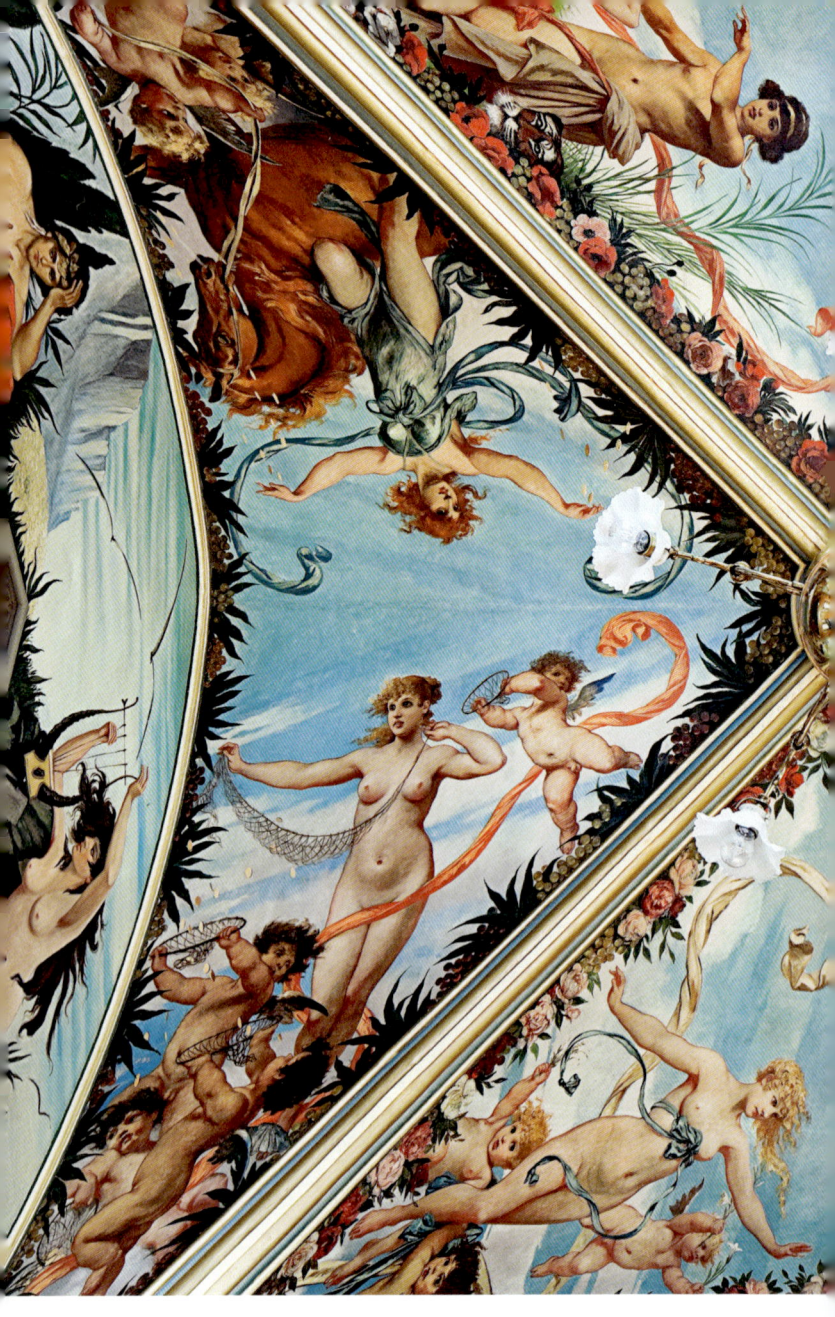

Hermann Schneider, paintings in the vault of the Tavern Room

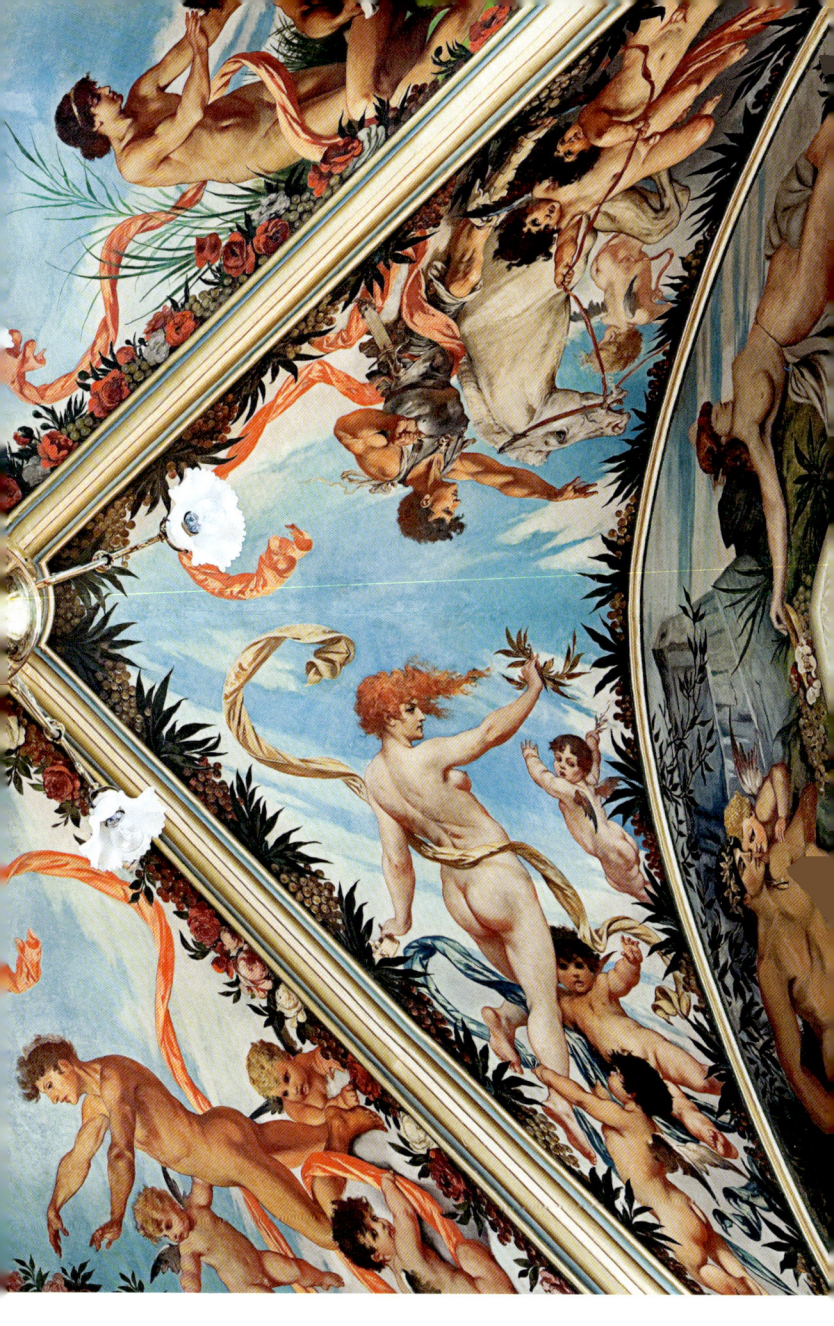

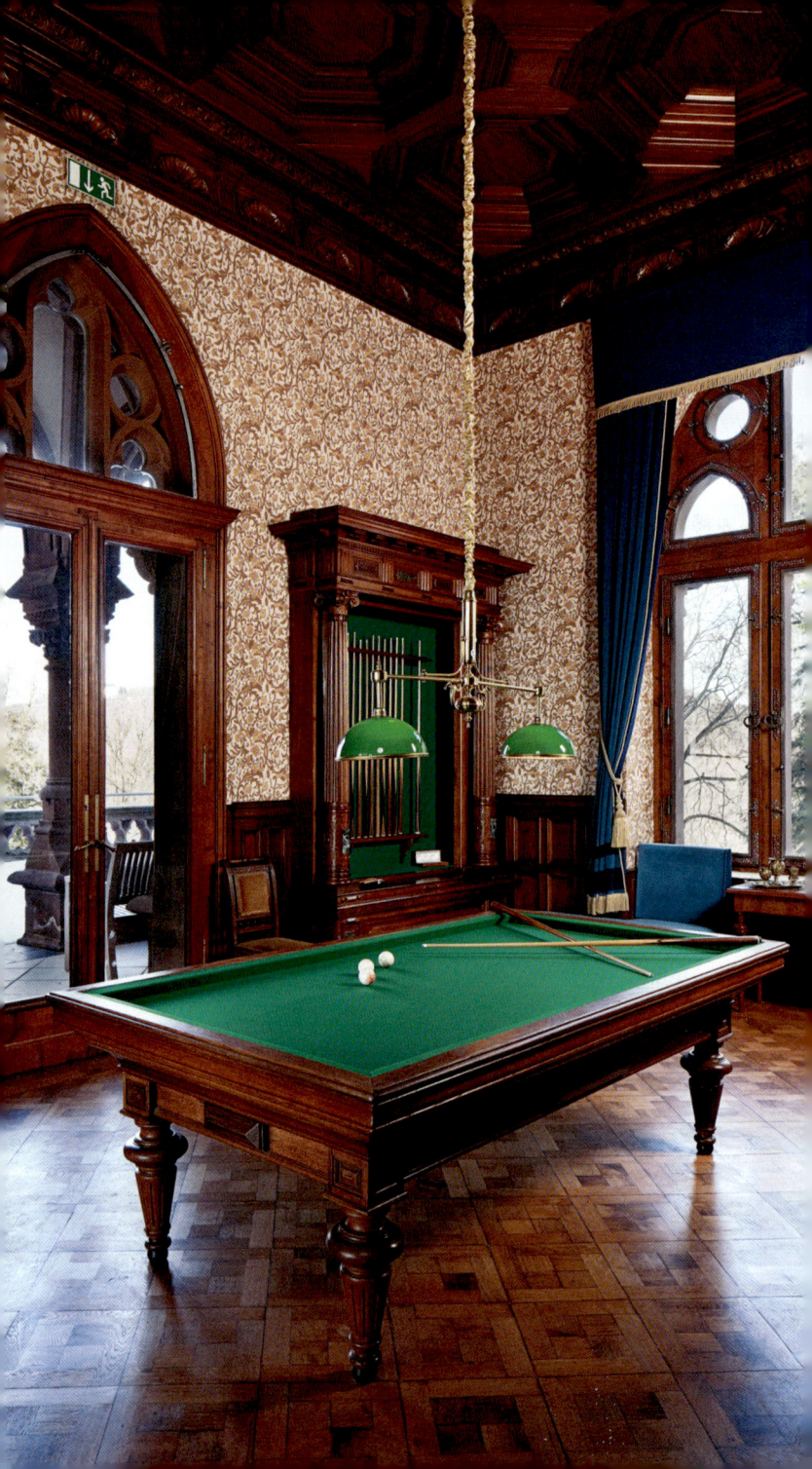

THE INTERIORS

Billiard Room

A larger room adjacent to the Art Gallery is defined by a large billiard table in the middle, which, like all non-fixed interior pieces, was acquired in recent years (left image). It was created in the 1920s in France.

The queue cabinet, the rifle cupboard, and the fake fireplace are immovable fixtures and were created by the Cologne company Pallenberg, as were the ceiling and wall panelling, presumably according to plans by Franz Langenberg. The colourful, inlaid marble is noteworthy. The forms are austere and are inspired by the ornamentation of the late Renaissance. Also of note are the very wide, mitred mouldings surrounding the octagonal panels on the ceiling. The designer did not make it easy for the carpenter.

The Billiard Room leads onwards to the Dancing Terrace, a large area from which an open stairway leads down to a terrace encompassing the entire castle. During festivities on warm summer nights, the easily accessible open area is and was certainly well suited for dancing.

Library

Stylistically the Billiard Room and the directly connected Library create one unit (image p. 65). The massive book cupboard reflects the austere, "old German" style, influenced by motifs from the late German Renaissance (image p. 83).

On the wall opposite the book cupboard, hangs an oil sketch by Friedrich von Keller, who drew this in preparation for his mural *Transfer of the Cologne Cathedral's Cornerstone* in the Main Stairwell in 1884 (image above). The books in the cupboard are a collection that might be representative of a typical library of

THE INTERIORS

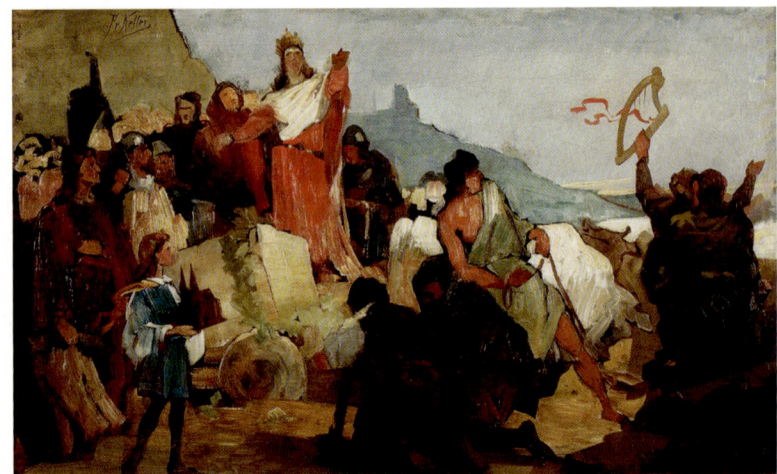

Friedrich Keller, Oil sketch for a painting in the Main Stairwell

the Gründerzeit; they have been acquired from rare and used book shops. The forty volumes of the *Rhenish Antiquarius*, however, are marked with the stamp of Schloss Drachenburg and as such have been returned to their original home.

The queue, rifle, and book cupboards all seem like accessories for a man of stature, who has them on display, as expected, but does not really need them. This becomes clear in the planning of an office in Stephan von Sarter's private apartment, in the same location but one story up. If he had ever resided in his palace, then this is surely where he would have kept literature pertinent to his work as an author and publisher.

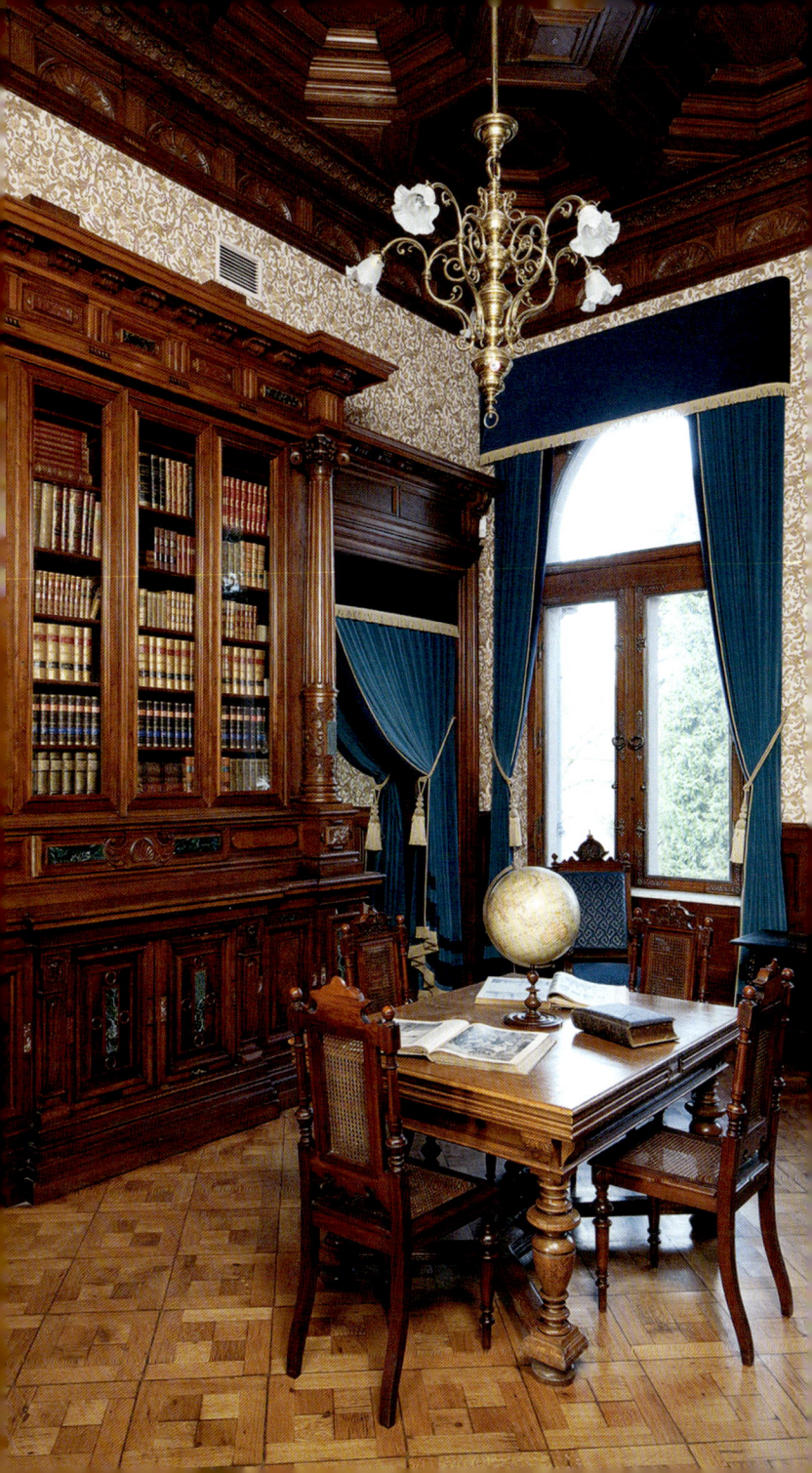

THE INTERIORS

Music Hall

The Music Hall is accessible directly from the Main Stairwell in the same location in the layout as the Reception Hall, but a bit smaller than the latter: The bay window downstairs is a balcony above. Its mosaic floor is inspired by Romanesque examples depicting ornamental dragon motifs (image p. 68). Above its entrance, the festively vaulted hall has a balcony, attached to which is Stephan von Sarter's crest, previously seen on the Northern Tower. Like the organ's casing on the balcony, it was added by the last private owner, Paul Spinat (right image).

The elaborate wainscoting was designed by Franz Langenberg, based on examples from around 1500. It was executed by the company J. Vershoven Nachfahren in Bonn. Elaborately decorated reticulated vaulting spans the room. The unusually formed Glockenflügel is the one that Hubert Biesenbach acquired from the manufacturing company Rud. Ibach Sohn in 1909. After the instrument was sold in 1938 by St. Michael's School, it was repurchased in 2001 with the help of the Verein der Freunde und Förderer von Schloss Drachenburg.

Jib Doors

Upon closer observation, hidden doors that have been discreetly integrated into the walls can be found in most of the rooms in Schloss Drachenburg. They allowed the staff to come and go, swiftly carrying out their work in narrow side stairwells and work rooms. One of these is in the corner between the Dining and Hunting Rooms. A spiral staircase leads from here to the hallway of the Guest-of-Honour Quarters.

The largest area of activity for the service personnel, however, was the bottom floor with its central kitchen and a variety of related rooms. The Front Building was also the realm of the servants. Up to its restoration, it had no sanitation or central heating

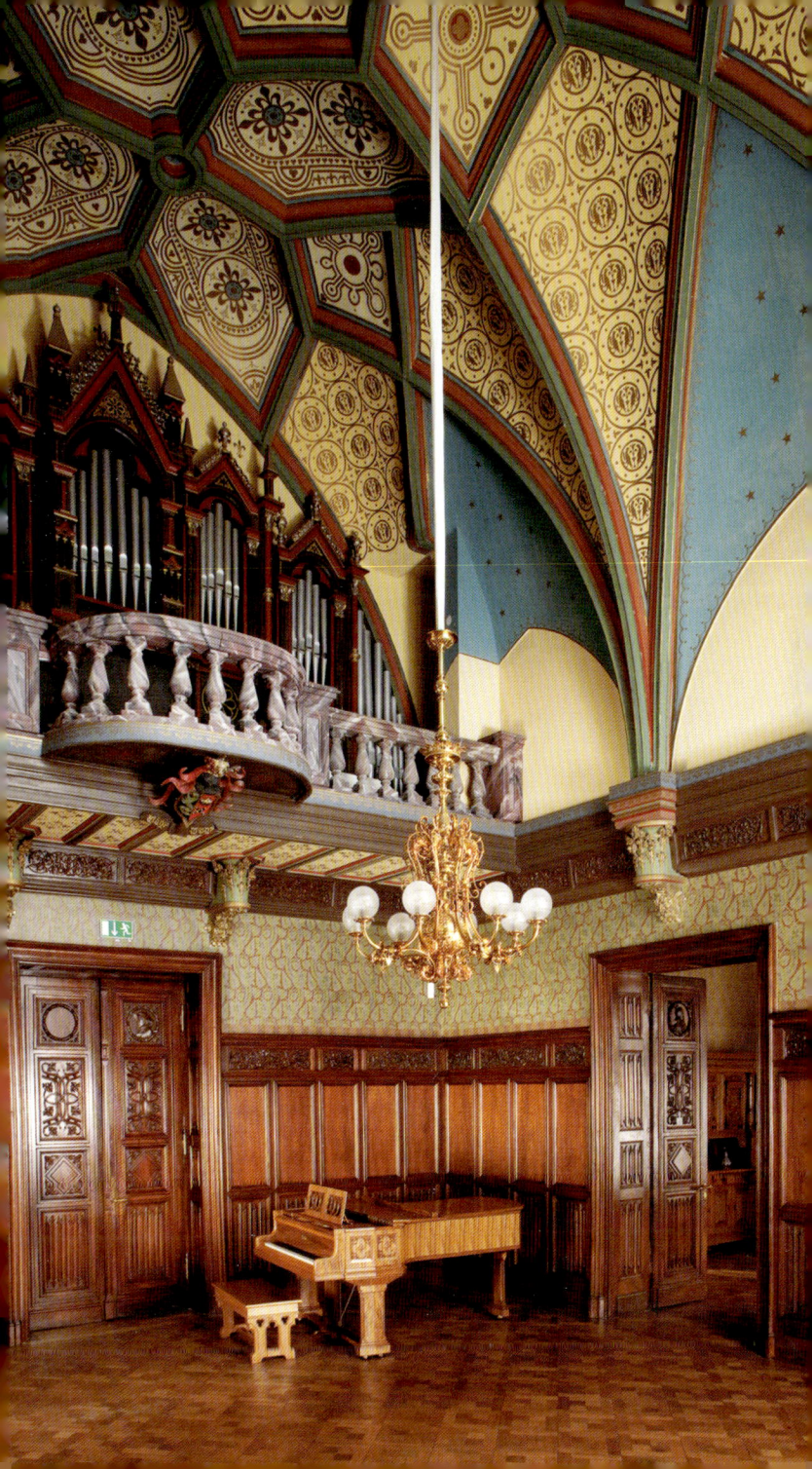

THE INTERIORS

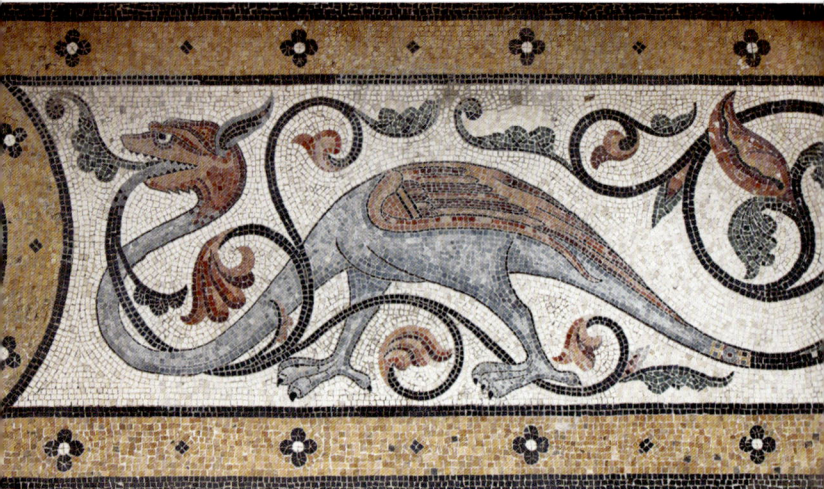

Balcony of the Music Hall, floor mosaic

On the upper floor, the Music Hall is the only room intended for festivities. All other rooms are more private in character, intended as the owner's residence and for select guests staying overnight. None of the original furnishings remain. Historic photographs were available, based on which historical furniture was purchased and the wallpaper and curtains were reconstructed. In one case, pieces of wallpaper were found behind the baseboards, which provided valuable information on the character and the patterns of the lost wall coverings.

THE INTERIORS

Private Residential Quarters

The Private Quarters offer a spacious bedroom with a large window facing east and a balcony along the full length of the room on the northern side above the Dancing Terrace. Between the bedroom and the private study, there is a small dressing room. Today, the private study is unfortunately taken over by an elevator, the price of making the castle handicap accessible. The existence of the private study testifies to the representative quality of the library one floor below.

The painting in the small hallway was originally located in the master bedroom (image p. 70). It was sold by a later proprietor. The model for the painting on porcelain by Carl Meinelt

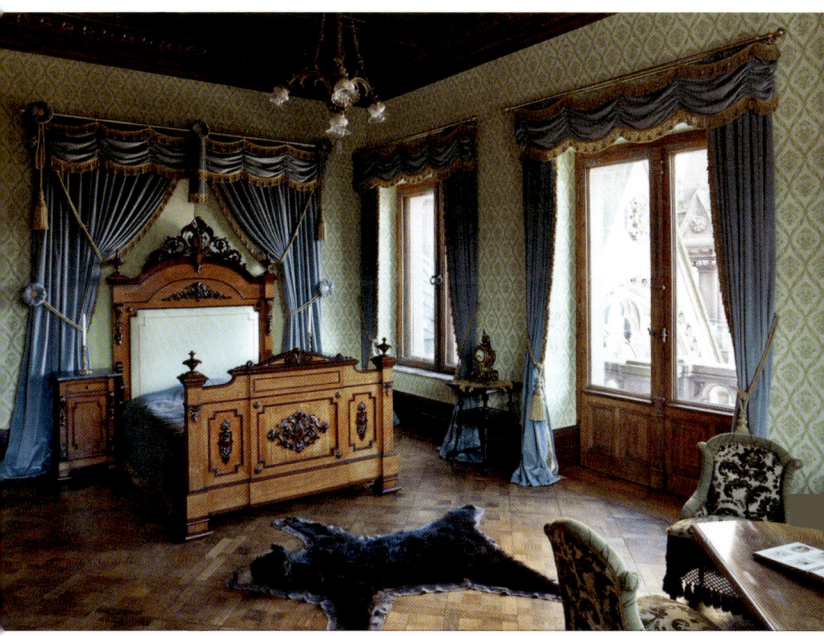

Private Bedroom

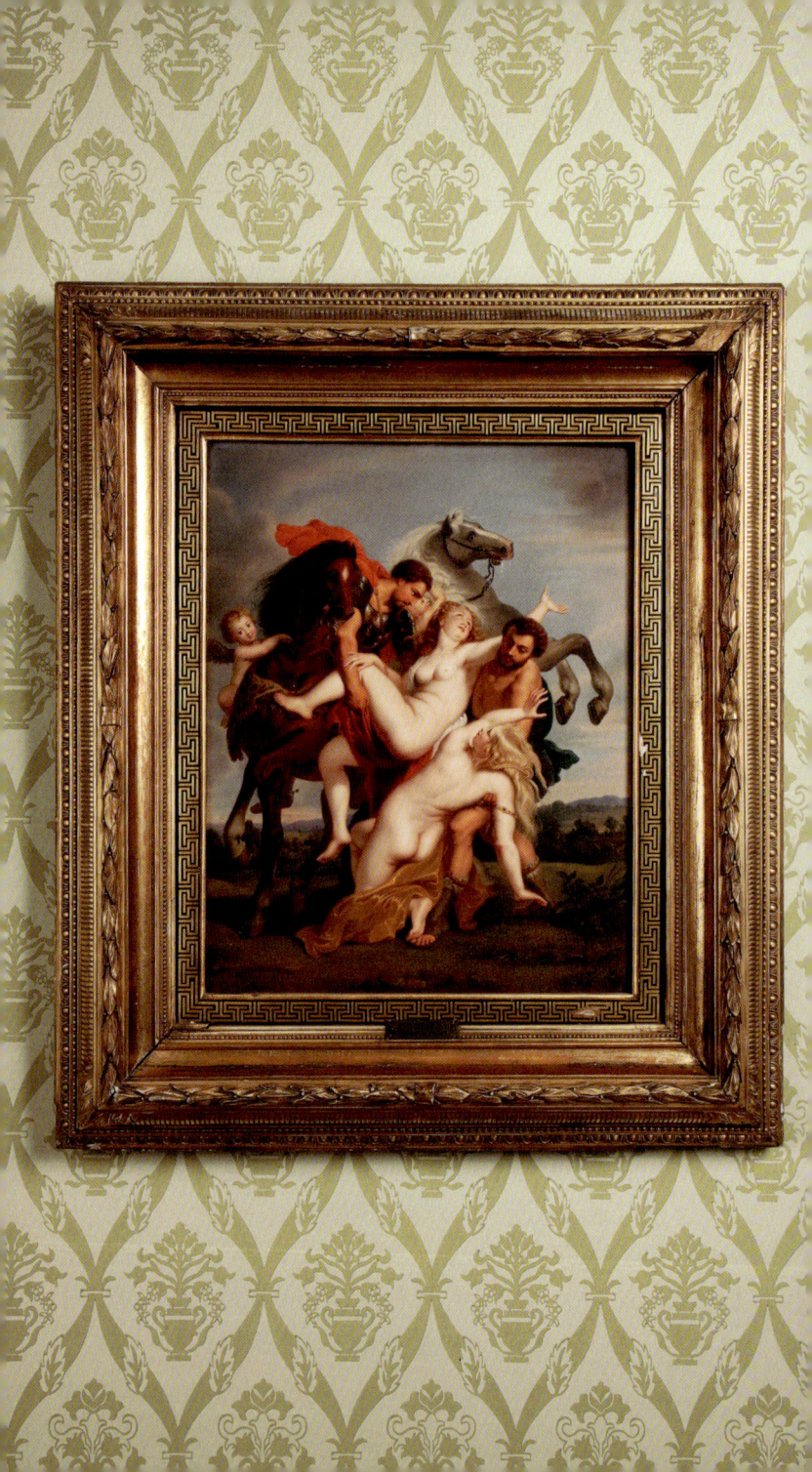

THE INTERIORS

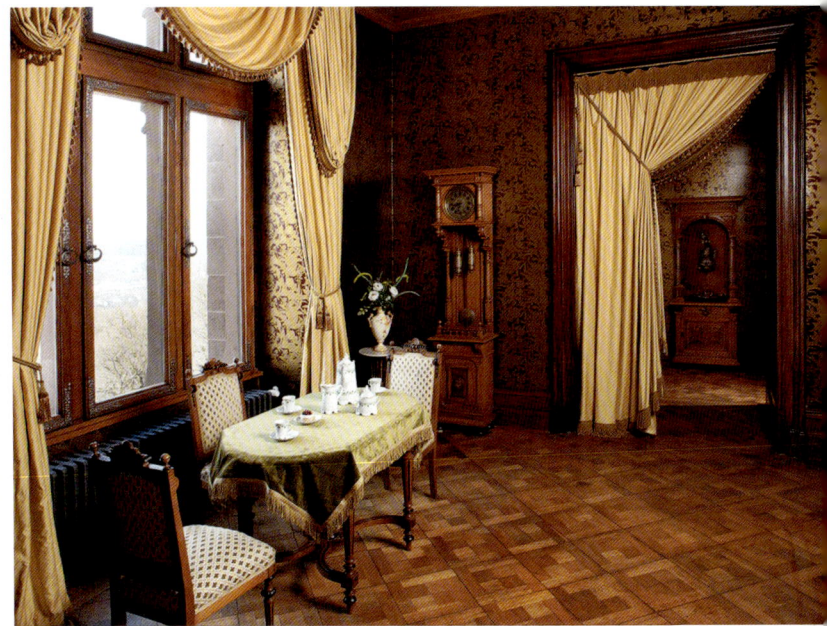

Breakfast Room

(1825–1900) is a painting by Peter Paul Rubens from the year 1618 that is in the Alte Pinakothek in Munich. The topic is the abduction of the daughters of Leucippus by Castor and Pollux. In 2002, the painting was bought back from a private collector.

By way of a small side room, which has a washbasin by the company Pallenberg from Cologne, the company that also contributed to the fixed interior furnishings in the representative spaces, one reaches the Breakfast Room (image above). The oil sketch on the wall shows the eastern wall in the Dining Room and is a loan from the Siebengebirgsmuseum Königswinter.

Carl Meinelt, The Rape of the Daughter of Leucippus, painting on porcelain after Rubens

THE INTERIORS

Guest-of-Honour Quarters

The main rooms of the Guest-of-Honour Quarters face west and south. This means the guests are being given the most spectacular view of the Rhine. The living room is furnished with pieces from the late nineteenth century. Above a red, upholstered bench hangs an oil sketch by Frank Kirchbach. It depicts the Nibelung Room with its murals of the fight between Brunhild and Kriemhild in front of the Worms Cathedral (image p. 74).

The bright wall-covering and the white furniture might not initially be associated with the period of Historicism. But there are image sources from the time around 1900 that confirm exactly this interior decor. The view from the toilet-oriel is exquisite (image p. 75).

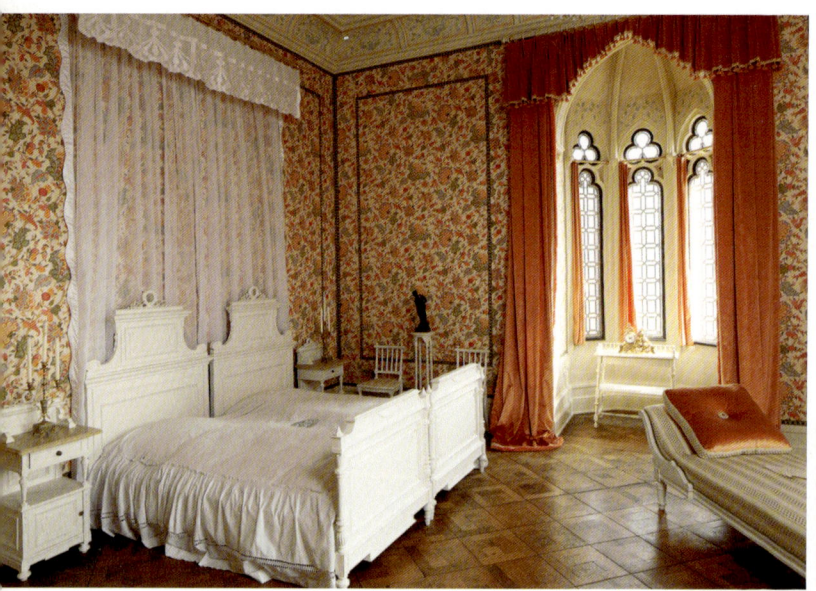

Guest-of-Honour Bedroom

Guest-of-Honour Living Room

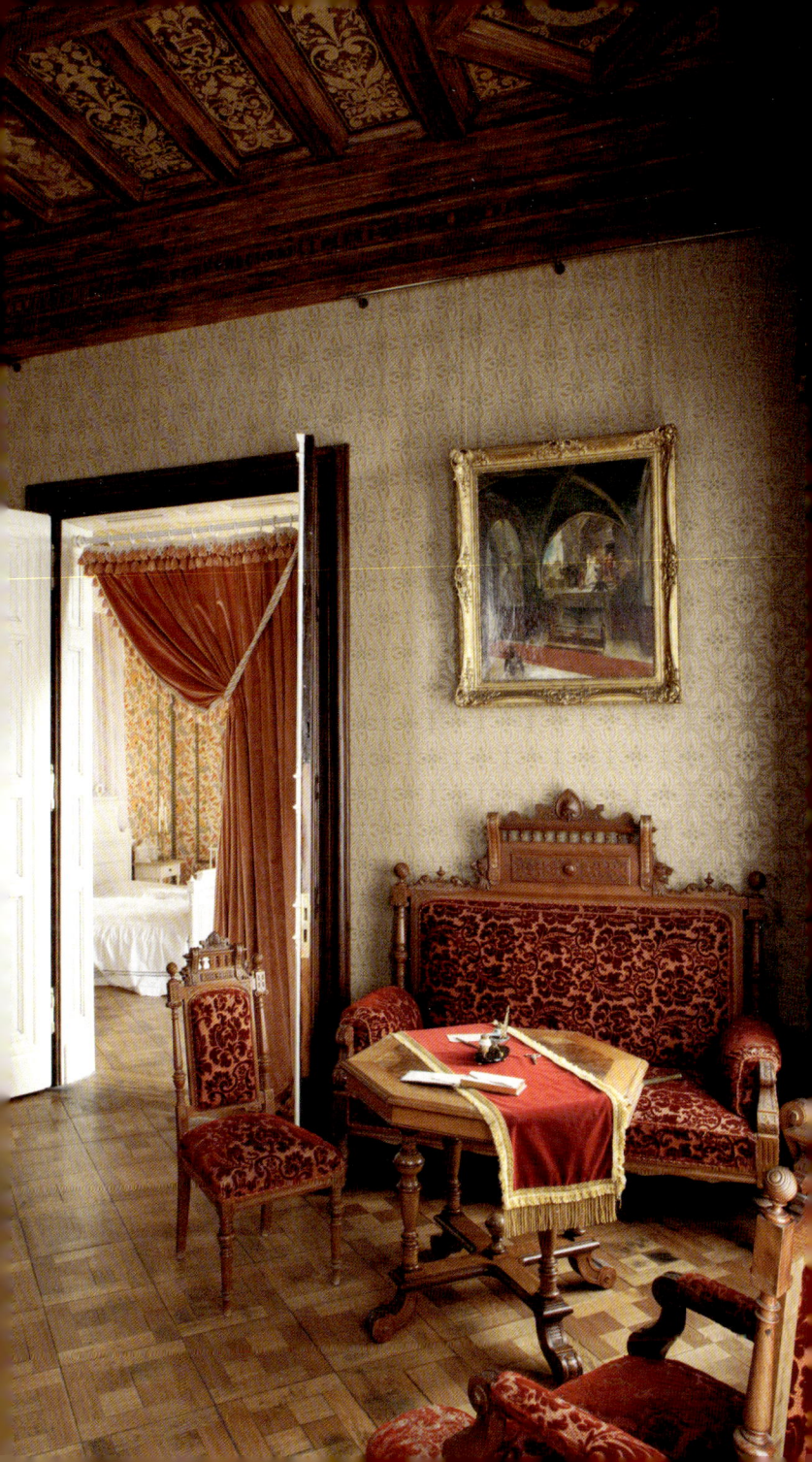

THE INTERIORS

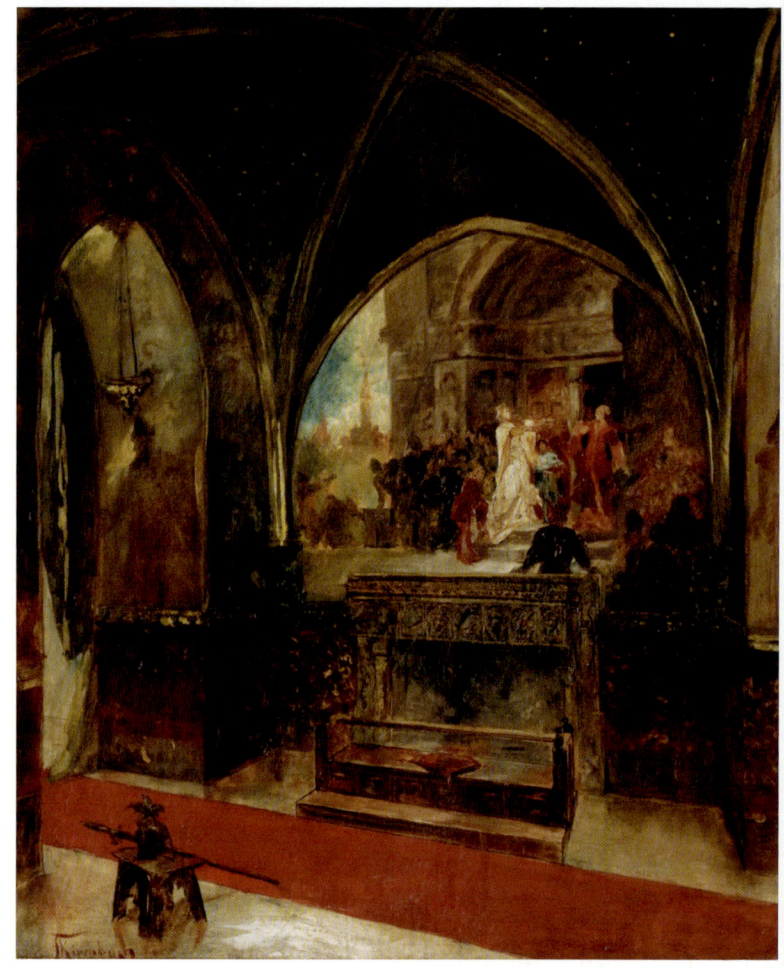

Frank Kirchbach, sketch for the design of the Nibelung Room

Toilet-oriel in the Guest-of-Honour Bedroom

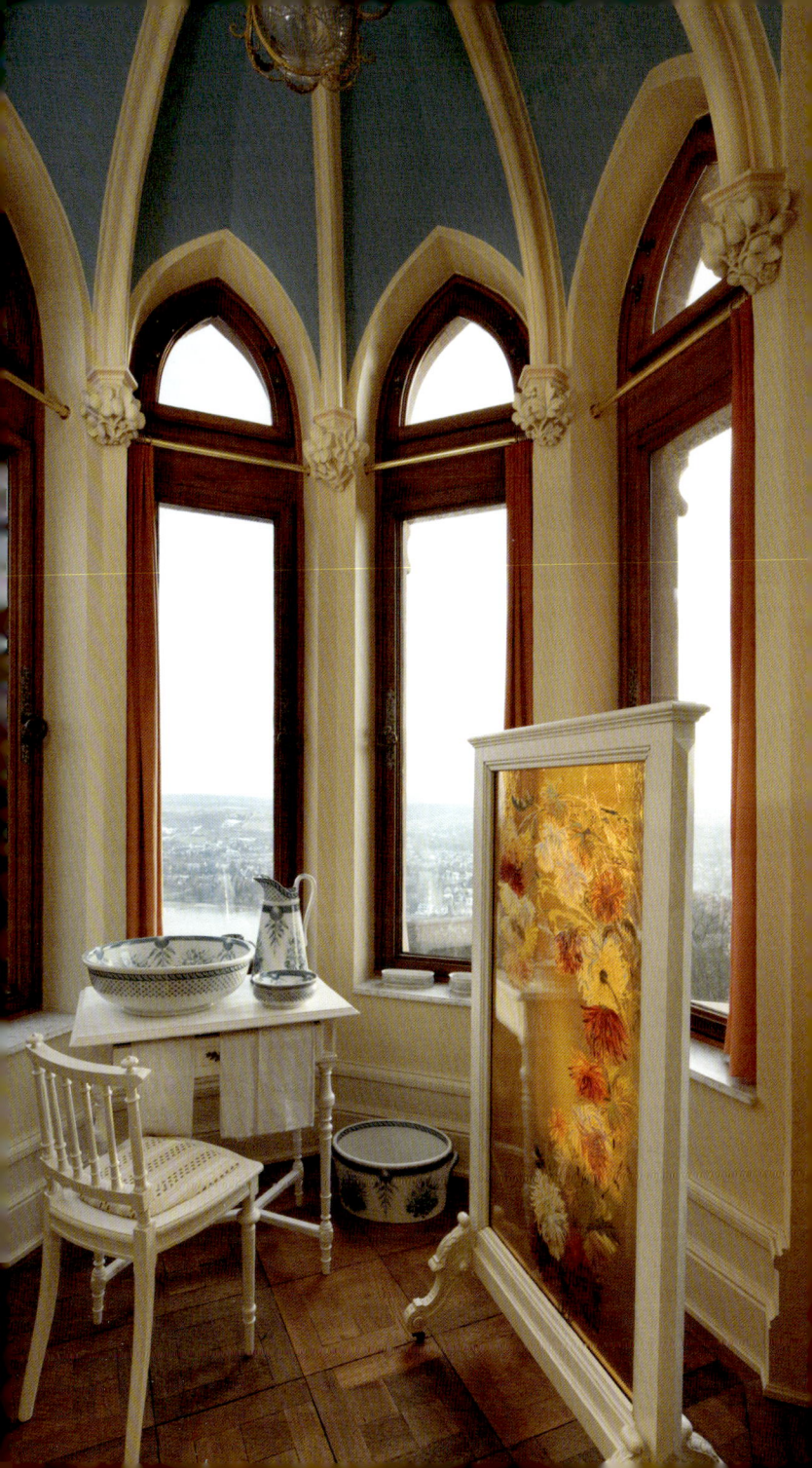

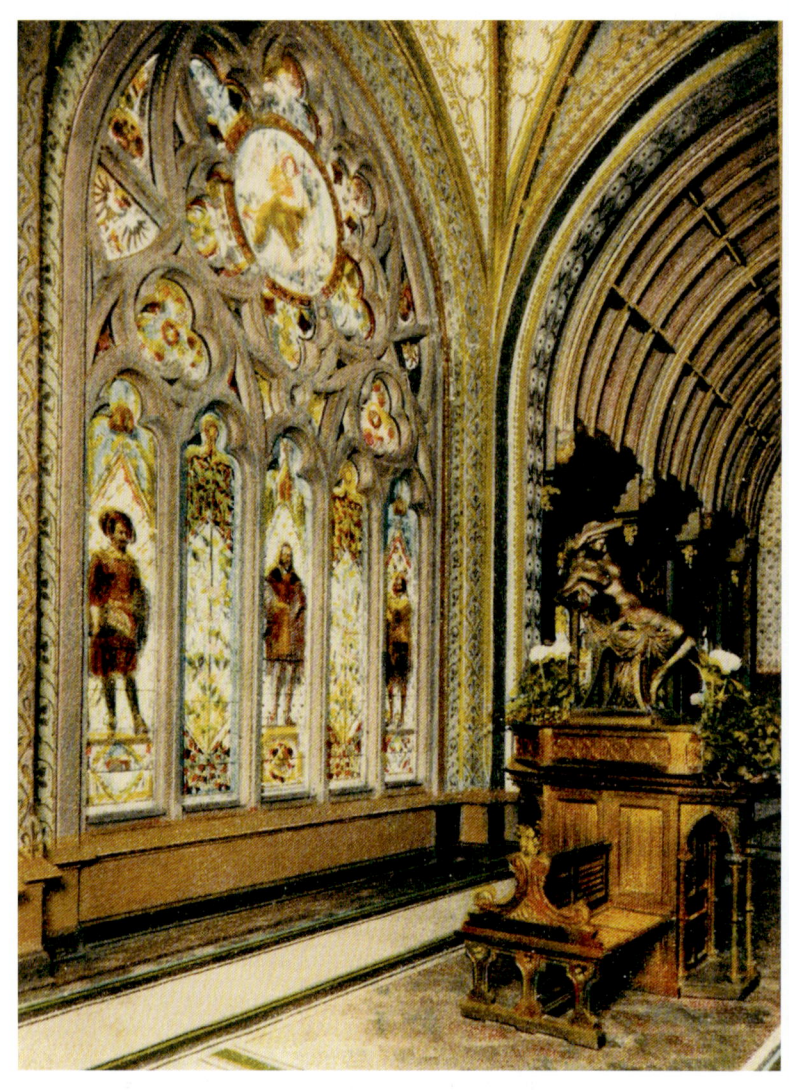

Window in the Art Gallery, 1903 postcard

THE HISTORY OF
THE DRACHENBURG

When Stephan von Sarter died in Paris in 1902, the childless bachelor left his fortune to relatives in the Rhineland. None of these had any particular interest in Schloss Drachenburg. Only Stephan von Sarter's sister's son, Dr. Jacob Hubert Biesenbach, a lawyer from Bonn, had any inclination to become the new lord of the castle. He paid his joint heirs 390,000 Marks in order to become the sole owner of the estate. His goal was to turn Schloss Drachenburg into a tourist attraction. He had "Nordic Summer Homes" built in the park for vacationing visitors. The picture series and postcards he had published at the time became important image sources for the restoration and repair (image on the left and p. 78). The Music Hall was used for public concerts. But the income was not sufficient to cover the considerable costs.

In 1910, Biesenbach sold the castle to retired cavalry captain Egbert von Simon who approached the economic aspect much more resolutely. Art exhibits, an open-air stage, and a minstrel contest were just a few of his ideas for achieving financial success. Conscripted during the First World War, Egbert von Simon was killed in a battle at Arras.

The businessman Hermann Flohr, who had become wealthy through, among other things, the sale of weapons, bought the entire complex – little by little – at various auctions. He resided in parts of the Drachenburg, leaving the remaining parts and the summerhouses available free of charge for the establishment of a women's convalescent home. In 1930, Flohr sold the Drachenburg under false pretences and with the help of empty promises made to the Christian Brothers, who established the St. Michael's Boarding School here. A large portion of the non-fixed furnishings tended to be impractical for their purposes and was consequently auctioned off at Lempertz in Cologne. The Art Hall became the chapel; the Tavern Room was turned into the sacristy.

THE HISTORY OF THE DRACHENBURG

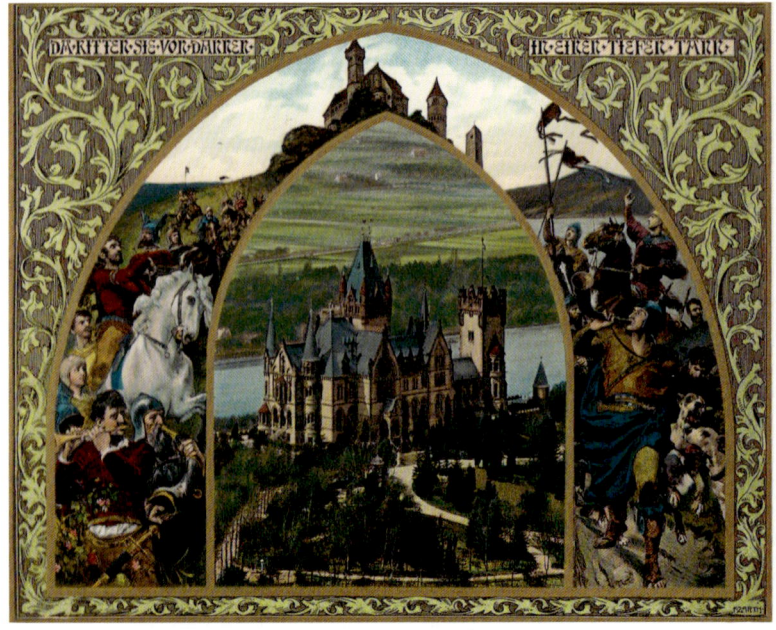

Wall painting on the west wall of the Nibelung Room and bird's eye view from the southeast, colour lithography, ca. 1905

The Catholic school faced growing difficulties with the Nazis. In 1938 the boarding school had to be closed. The Christian Brothers sold the castle in 1940 to the German Labour Front, which in turn established the Adolf Hitler School in its place. The most serious changes during the Second World War were the modification of the Main Entrance, military structures in the landscape park, and finally the shell bombardment, as a result of which the Art Hall's dome and almost all of the stained glass were destroyed.

After the war, the state of North Rhine-Westphalia was the Drachenburg's owner. Initially, it was rented out to the German Reich Railway and later the Federal Railway division at Wuppertal as a training facility, until they found a permanent home in the

THE HISTORY OF THE DRACHENBURG

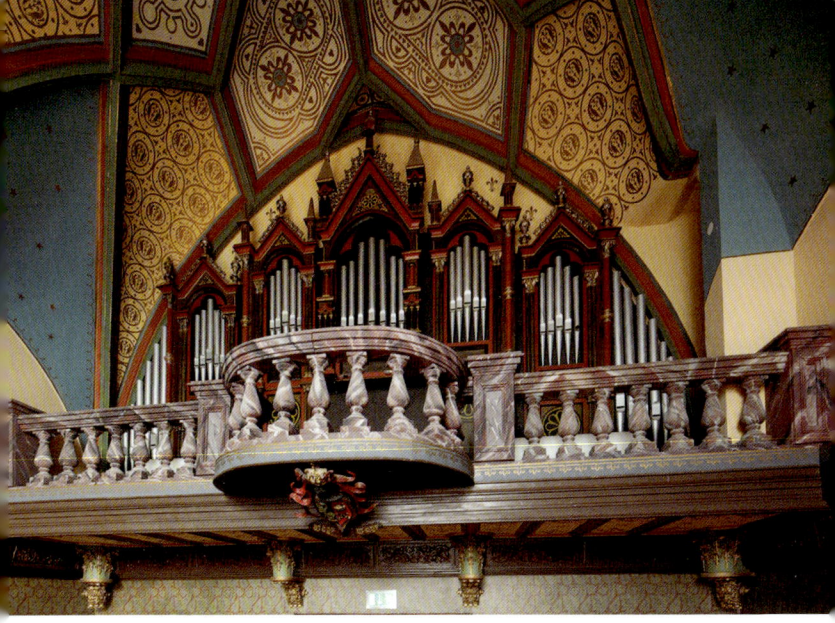

Organ in Music Hall

Wuppertal district in 1959. Schloss Drachenburg now stood empty and increasingly fell into disrepair: the castle became the venue for many a party, with all murals within reach subject to destruction, the parquet floors serving as firewood, and the air thick with the sweet, heady smell of weed. Meanwhile, the property management administration was planning its demolition.

But already in 1963, the "Syndicate for the Preservation of the Drachenburg" was founded, which succeeded in getting the state of North Rhine-Westphalia to classify the castle as worthy of preservation.

Its purchase by the textile merchant Paul Spinat from Bad Godesberg in 1971 was a turn for the better. He wanted the castle as a castle. He used it for celebrations, but also opened it for visitors again. And he brought along enthusiasm, energy, imagination, and, last but not least, plenty of money. It was the result of his dedication that the castle was fully and sustainably restored under the management of the North Rhine-Westphalia Foundation from 1989–2010. Even now, after the successful completion of the restoration in 2010, there are still traces from the "Spinat Era". His "court painter" Peter Tutzauer took care of reconstructing damaged murals and created some completely anew. He signed his works in the doorjambs of the Nibelung Room. The fake organ in the Music Hall will remain as a memorial to this bustling owner (image p. 79).

Paul Spinat died in 1989, deeply in debt, and in the last moment the state of North Rhine-Westphalia took advantage of its right of pre-emption. With this, a long phase of consolidation began. Investigations were done of the basic structure, as well as evaluations of necessary measures for conserving it. Concepts for its use in the interest of the public fill countless binders in a great variety of offices. The restoration process took 20 years in which public input was not lacking. And with more than respectable results.

Today the North Rhine-Westphalia Foundation owns the Drachenburg. And thus, the palace's future is safe.

Peter Fuchs, Emperor Wilhelm I on the south facade

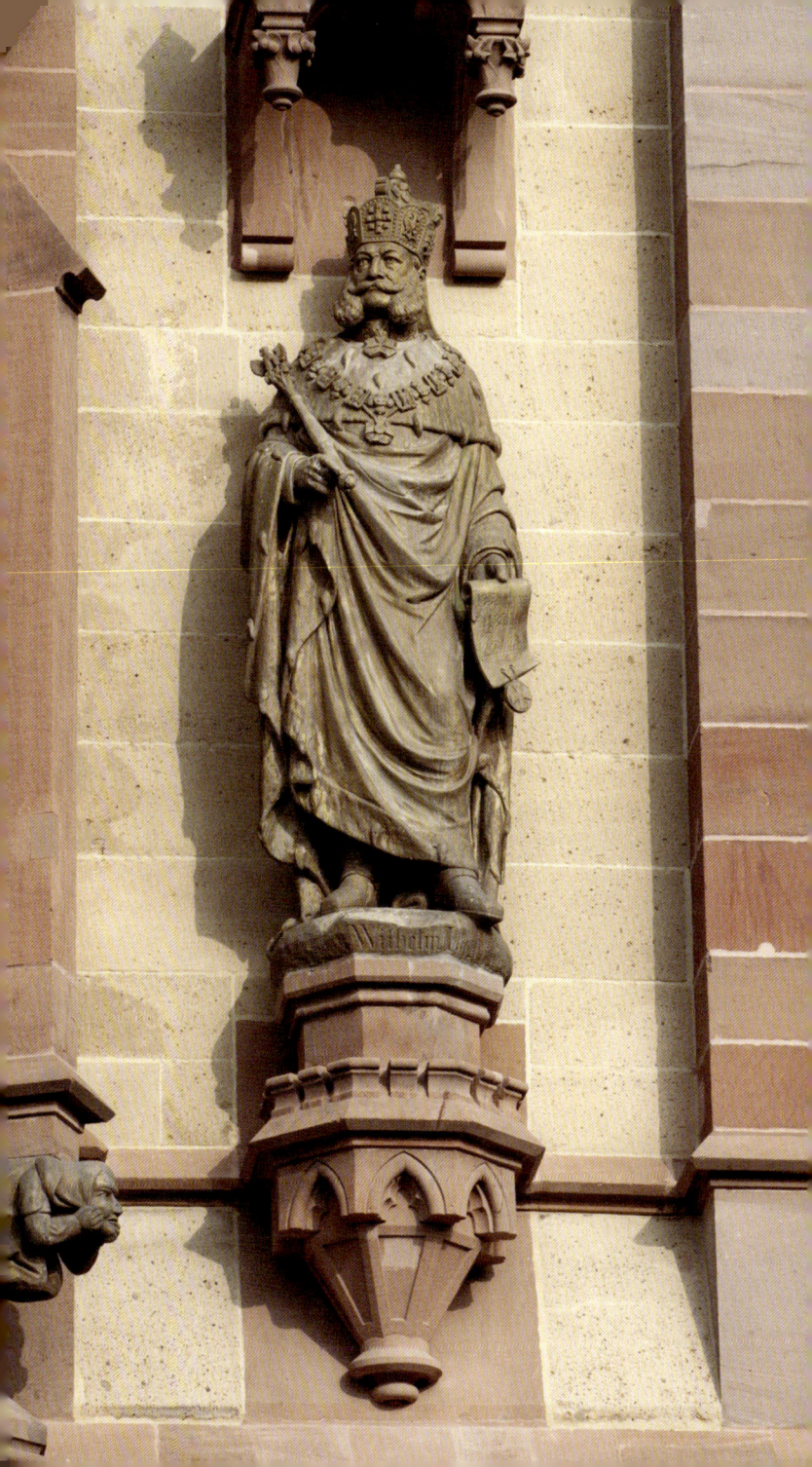

THE MONUMENT
SCHLOSS DRACHENBURG

Stephan von Sarter gave his Rhenish home a memorial to his patriotic sentiments in the form of Schloss Drachenburg. The statues of emperors (image p. 37 and 81) and the Hohenzollern variation of the imperial eagle, presented so strikingly on his castle, bear witness to the owner's allegiance to the state. This patriotism can also be seen in the murals on the castle's inside, as for example the enthroned emperors in the stairwell.

But also the Drachenfels's close proximity played an essential role in the paintings chosen for the interior decoration of the castle. The murals in the Dining Room with their hunting scenes are closely tied to the Drachenfels. Also, the topics chosen for the Main Stairwell seem to make clear connections to the owner's Rhenish home. With the depictions of the "Minstrel's contest on the island Nonnenwerth", the "Transport of the Cornerstone to the Cologne Cathedral", and others, events are being referenced that could have been observed from the Drachenburg, had it existed at the time. The building's axes are aligned with the Cologne Cathedral on the horizon. Cologne churches are used as identifiable elements in the murals.

Through the localization of the dragon battle from the Nibelung Saga, it becomes the theme for the building's iconography, with the "dragon slayer" at the main entrance and in the murals of one room. The "dragon virgin" on a gable of the western façade, however, is derived from a different, more local context of the tales about fire-spitting lindworms.

Especially the lost stained glass in the Art Gallery emphasized the owner's universal education, which was expressed in the pointed veneration of the generally recognized characters that had become part of the canon of cultural history. In the Wilhelminian period, there was no doubt about the significance

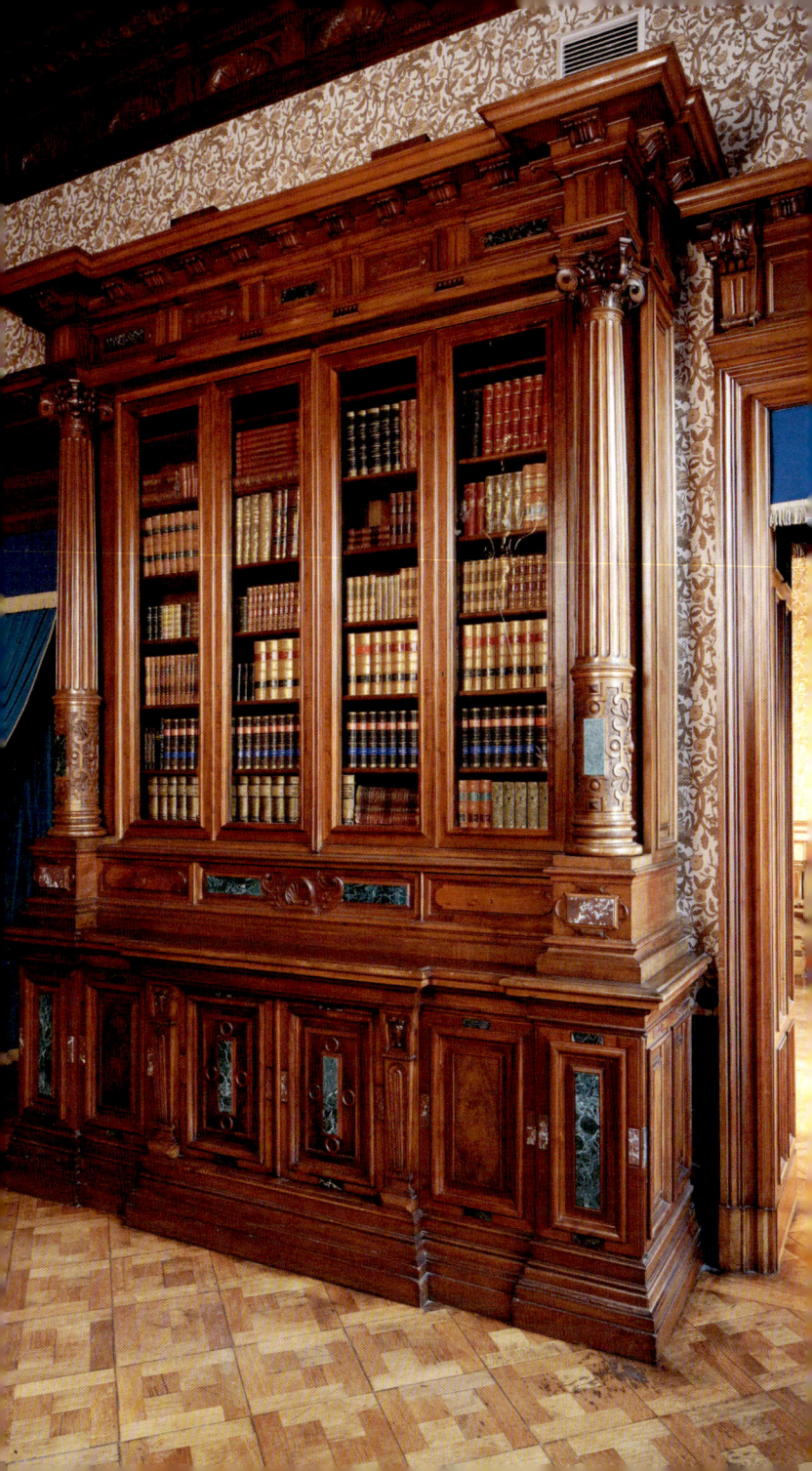

The Monument Schloss Drachenburg

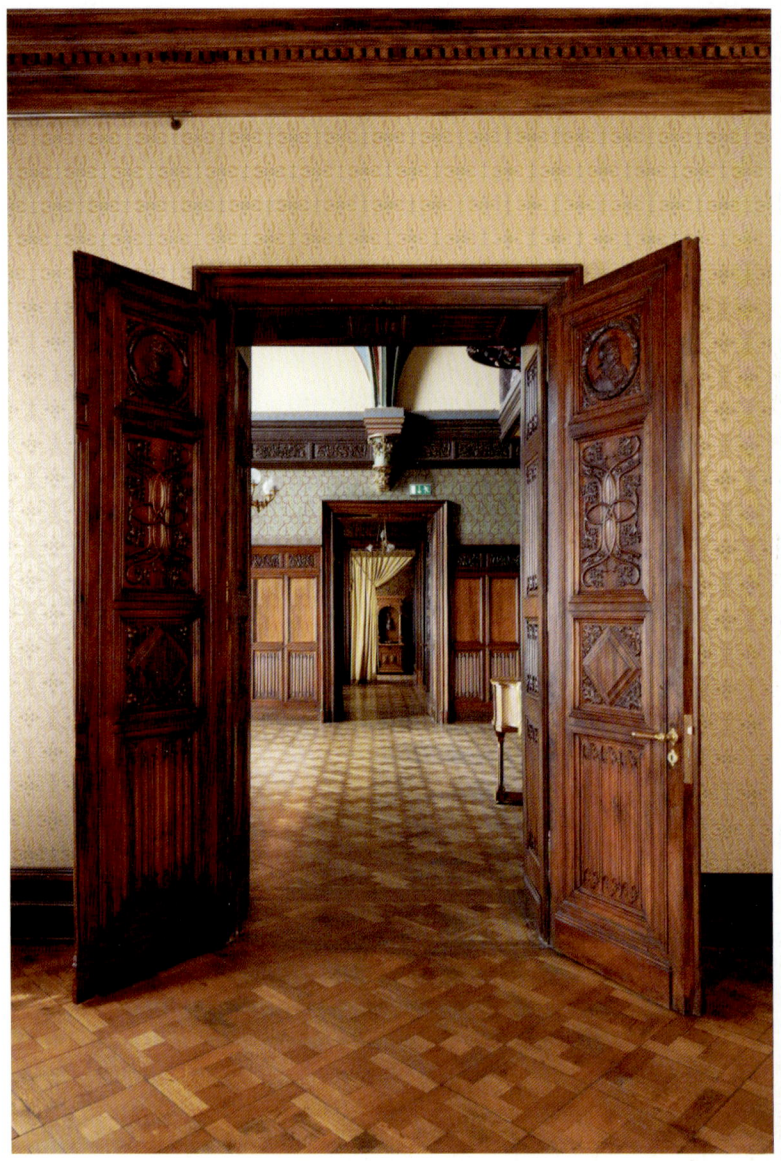

View from the Guest-of-Honour living room, through the Music Hall and the Breakfast Room to the Lavatory of a side room of the private apartments

Faux-fireplace in the Billiard Room

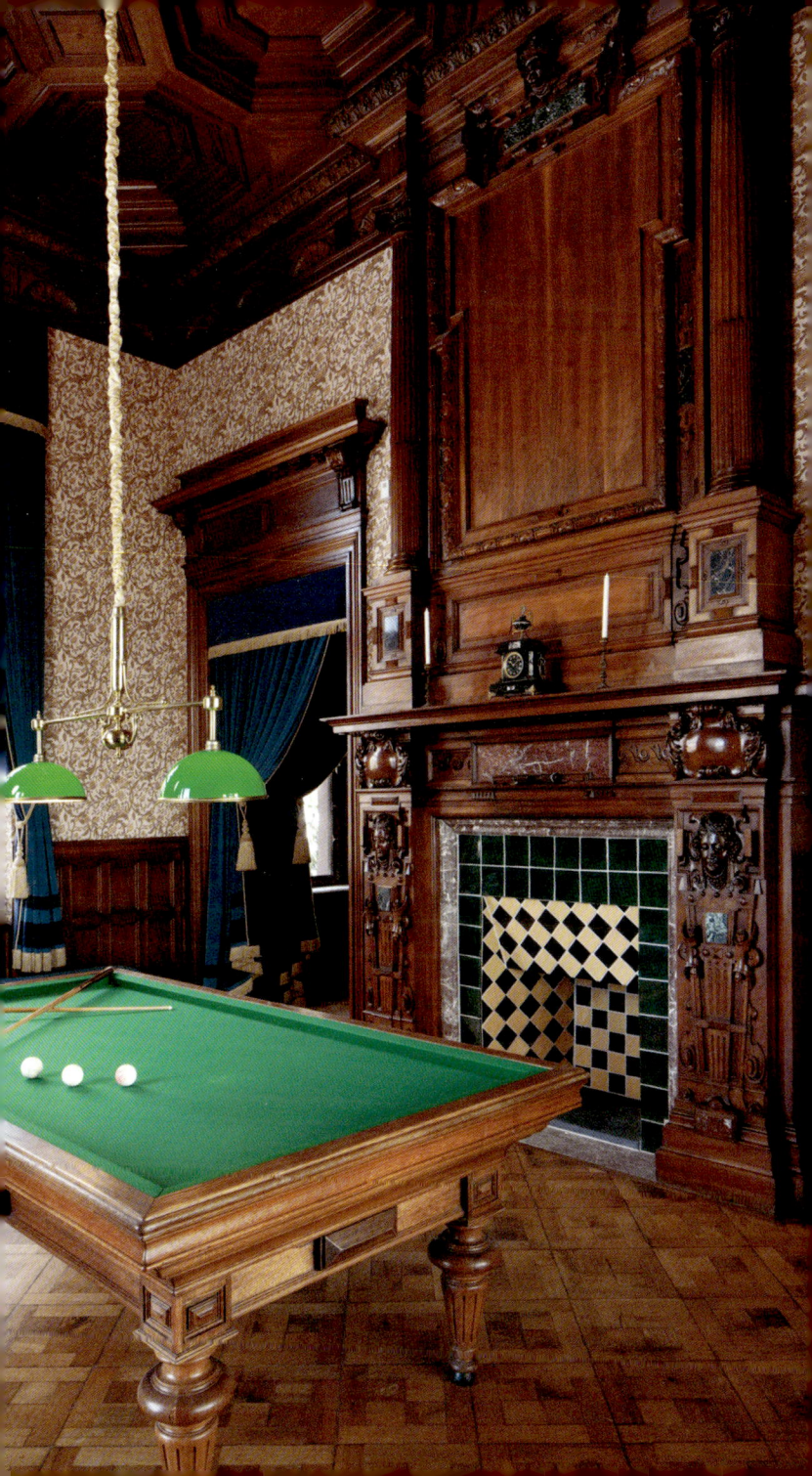

The Monument Schloss Drachenburg

of Albrecht Dürer, Peter Vischer, Wolfram von Eschenbach, and Gerhards von Rile. The placement their statues high up on the Northern Tower was certainly no manifestation of an avant-garde disposition.

The Drachenburg's complete lower floor had a representative function for the owner. A bust of Apollo signified his appreciation of art, paintings with bacchanalian topics in a somewhat remote small room stood for Rhenish gaiety with its affinity for men's jokes. The man of the world presented himself with cabinets for rifles, queues, and books (image p. 83) as though these were being crossed off from a list of accoutrements needed to be member of the haute-bourgeoisie. Schloss Drachenburg's architecture is highly contradictory.

The outside is puzzling (image p. 92). The structure's lavish decoration and the wealth of different shapes seen in the roofscape are definitely not apt to reveal the meaning and function of individual rooms to the viewer. Some of the detail found on the exterior has no equivalent on the inside and remains purely a façade.

In defiance of what the picturesque exterior might suggest, the structure of the rooms inside is well organized. The enfilades of the series of rooms are of Baroque rationality (image p. 84). Technically, at the end of the nineteenth century, the building was at the forefront of its time. The residents and their guests were offered all the comforts imaginable. The fireplaces are purely aesthetic and non-functional (image p. 85) There was – and is – central heating.

As such, the building is as much of a riddle and as contradictory as its builder and owner Stephan von Sarter. He had the Duke of Sachsen-Meiningen bestow upon him the status of baron. He had a palace built for himself in his Rhenish home representing not only his intellectual status but also his national pride, but nevertheless remained in Paris and had himself naturalized as a French citizen.

View from the Northern Tower southwards to the Main Tower, in the background the Rhine and the Drachenfels

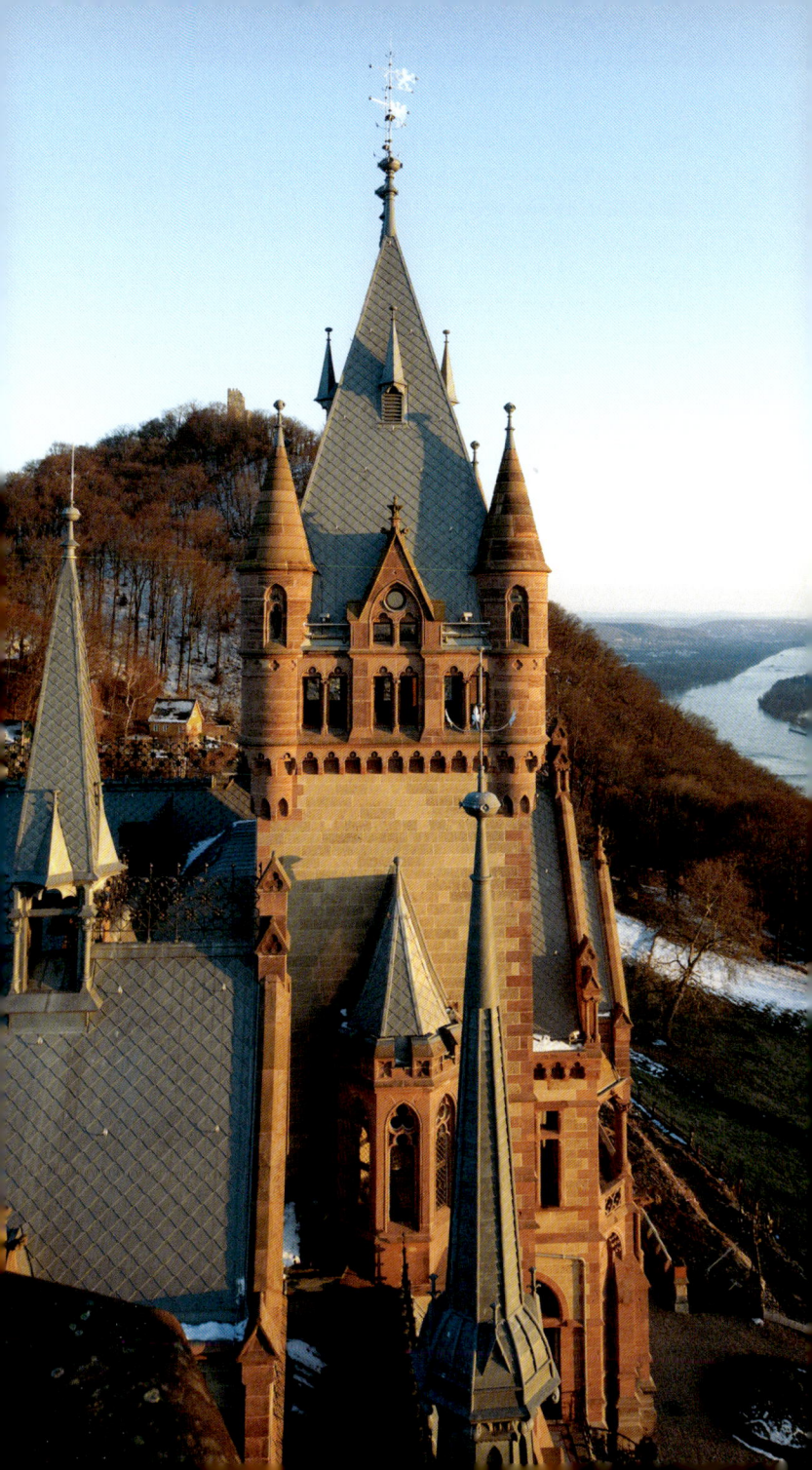

The NRW Foundation
Giving Nature, Culture, and Volunteer Work a Chance

Since its establishment in 1986, the North Rhine-Westphalia Foundation has combined under one roof supportive measures for both environmental conservation and the preservation of local traditions and culture. In this way, it is currently unique among similar foundations in Germany. But the constellation is not surprising if you consider the term "home" (*Heimat*) in its entirety: as the combination of nature and culture, as a "cultural landscape" that has evolved over hundreds or even thousands of years, which was formed by people human beings along with their history. Mills and industrial memorials are just as much as part of this as are castles, palaces, and aristocratic estates, archaeological monuments from Roman times, or highly modern museums on the history of the Romans. Manmade heath lands are the foundation's focus, but also industrial wastelands that are now often rehabilitated as natural spaces. With the shallow Lower Rhine, the fertile Münsterland, and Central German Uplands in the Eifel, and in the Siegerland and Sauerland, NRW has a lot of varied natural environments to offer. The state's geographical and cultural variety are repeatedly described as being an advantage – for the people who live here, for whom North Rhine-Westphalia is a beloved home.

Preserving Natural and Cultural Heritage

Located in the state capital, the NRW Foundation has primarily been supporting volunteer clubs, associations, and groups that have concrete projects for environmental conservation, and home and culture preservation, in NRW. So far, the NRW foundation has been able to support about 2300 measures – the most ambitious and elaborate of which, by far, is the restoration of Schloss Drachenburg in Königswinter. Aside from this, there are also other projects that are certainly of interest nationally: For example, the NRW Foundation built the Neanderthal Museum in

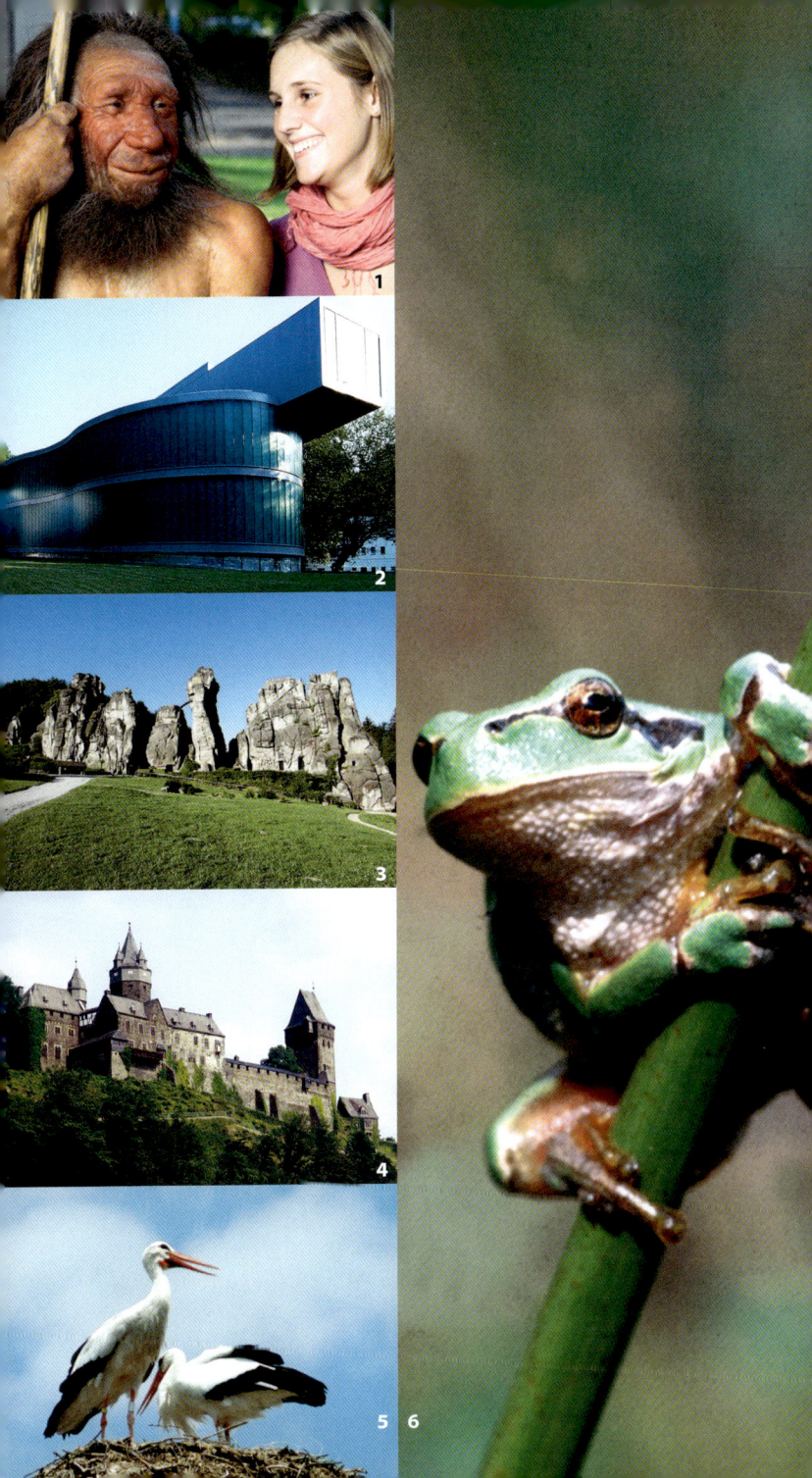

Mettmann (image 1,2), which attracts up to 200,000 visitors per year, including many from other countries as well. The legendary Externsteine (image 3) in Eastern Westphalia also attract hundreds of thousands of visitors yearly. With the help of the NRW Foundation, a new information centre is being built there. The Beethoven House in Bonn also benefited from the NRW Foundation, as did the Corvey Abbey in Höxter or the venerable Altena Castle (image 4), one of the prettiest hill castles in North Rhine-Westphalia. Additionally, the NRW Foundation has ensured the renovation or securing of countless old farm buildings, artisanry businesses, coal-mine complexes, and other, usually listed, structures that are then used as museums or for cultural events and are open to the public.

As for environmental conservation, there is a focus on the acquisition and maintenance of nature sanctuaries and areas worthy of protection. The North Rhine-Westphalia Foundation currently already owns about 6000 hectares of land: meadows and heaths, bogs, forests, and pastures. In this way, the habitat of endangered animals and plants can be protected and maintained for the future. The benefactors are, among others, the white storks in the Weser Hills (image 5), the colonies of greenbacks in Münsterland's Coesfeld (image 6), the daffodils growing wild in the Eifel's valleys near Monschau, and countless orchids in the Siegerland. Especially old farming landscapes like the meadows and the mountain pastures of the Lipper Höhe in Siegen-Burbach have a special standing. In these areas, culture and nature are inseparably interwoven.

A Matter of Honour

Many of the NRW Foundation's projects are backed by an incredible level of dedication on the part of volunteers who bring to the table passion and expertise, championing concrete measures. Thousands of hours of volunteer work are often invested in the restoration of historic buildings. The NRW Foundation gladly supports this commitment, because when something is done voluntarily, it is generally done with passion – and as such, people are working to preserve and care for their home, out of true conviction.

The NRW Foundation's funds are acquired through the returns on the endowment and from lottery income. But these resources are not sufficient to support the various, diverse projects that support nature, the homeland and its culture. Not all grant applications directed to the NRW Foundation can be approved. As a result, the NRW Foundation is appealing to people to get involved. About 8000 citizens are members of the Friends Association for the NRW Foundation. With their membership dues and donations, they support selected projects. Nature enthusiasts and local patriots support the foundation as they can with donations and personal involvement over the course of many years and some of them even do so in their last will, when they include the foundation or friends association in their testament. For over ten years now, the NRW Foundation has been allowing the establishment of dependent foundations. As the trustee, the NRW Foundation takes on the administrative tasks and supports projects as it can. And so, over the course of the past 25 years, an active family of foundations has formed, which continues to hope for still more support in order – together with the people of this state – to preserve, support, and create a desirable North Rhine-Westphalia for the future.

Winfried Raffel

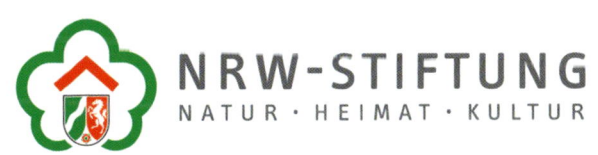

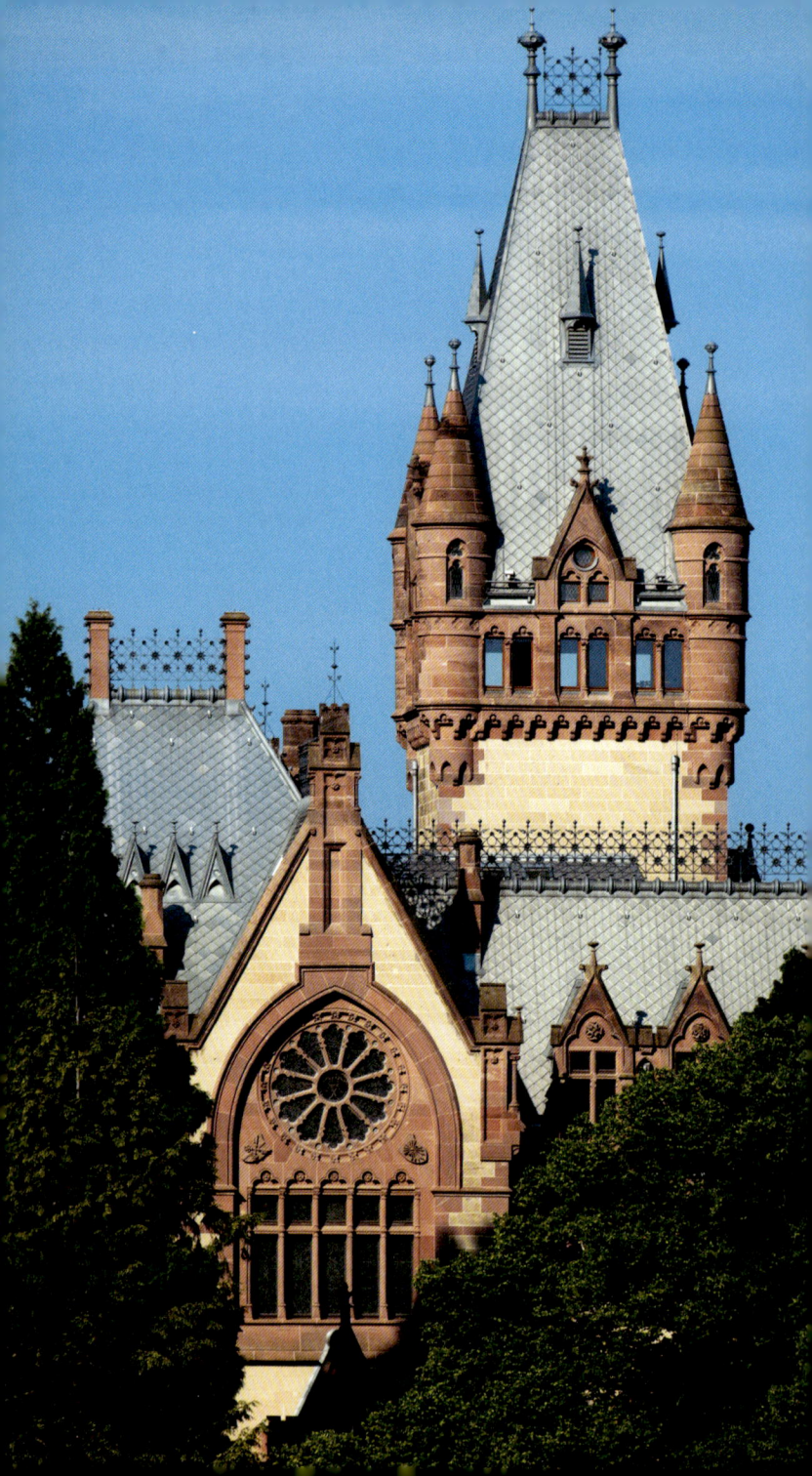